THE TRUTH ABOUT

PAY-PER-CLICK SEARCH ADVERTISING

Kevin Lee

Portions of this book originally appeared as columns written by Kevin Lee and published by Incisive Media's *The ClickZ Network* (www.click.com). Used with permission.

FT Press offers excellent discounts on this book when ordered in quantity for bulk purchases or special sales. For more information, please contact U.S. Corporate and Government Sales, 1-800-382-3419, corpsales@pearsontechgroup.com. For sales outside the U.S., please contact International Sales at international@pearsoned.com.

Printed in the United States of America

First Printing February 2009

ISBN-10: 0-7897-3832-5
ISBN-13: 978-0-7897-3832-5

Pearson Education LTD.
Pearson Education Australia PTY, Limited.
Pearson Education Singapore, Pte. Ltd.
Pearson Education North Asia, Ltd.
Pearson Education Canada, Ltd.
Pearson Educatión de Mexico, S.A. de C.V.
Pearson Education—Japan
Pearson Education Malaysia, Pte. Ltd.

Library of Congress Cataloging-in-Publication Data

Lee, Kevin.

The truth about search engine advertising / Kevin Lee.

   p. cm.

ISBN 978-0-7897-3832-5

1. Internet advertising. 2. Internet marketing. 3. Web search engines. I. Title.

HF6146.I58L438 2009

659.14'4--dc22

2008051425

Publisher
Paul Boger

Associate Publisher
Greg Wiegand

Acquisitions Editor
Rick Kughen

Development Editor
Rick Kughen

Technical Editor
Amanda Watlington

Technical Reviewer
Gordon Hotchkiss

Marketing Coordinator
Judi Taylor

Cover and Interior Design
Stuart Jackman,
Dorling Kindersley

Managing Editor
Kristy Hart

Senior Project Editor
Lori Lyons

Copy Editor
Water Crest Publishing, Inc.

Design Manager
Sandra Schroeder

Senior Compositor
Gloria Schurick

Proofreader
San Dee Phillips

Manufacturing Buyer
Dan Uhrig

Part I   The Truth About Why You Need Paid Placement SEM

Part II   The Truth About the History of Paid Search

Part III   The Truth About Google, Yahoo!, and Microsoft

Part IV   The Truth About Customer Acquisition, ROI, Profit, and ROAS

Part V   The Truth About Branding and Search

Part VI   The Truth About Technology and Analytics

Part VII The Truth About Best Practices

Part VIII The Truth About Optimizing Your Bids

Part IX The Truth About Landing Pages

Part X The Truth About Second-Tier Engines and Nonsearch Keyword-Targeted Media

Part XI The Truth About B2B Paid Search

Part XII The Truth About the Future of Keyword-Targeted Media

TRUTH

1

Paid placement search, supply, demand, and auctions

If you are a CMO (chief marketing officer), small business owner, agency, or in-house media planner/ buyer, chances are you have already added or will soon add paid placement search engine marketing (SEM) to your online marketing plans. As someone who most likely has bought many forms of advertising and media in the past, you approach search marketing from a unique perspective, defining search visibility and the resulting pay-per-click traffic as media. It is critical, however, to understand some of the ways that Pay Per Click (PPC) search media is unique, particularly in comparison to other types of online media. The following issues are particularly important when planning and buying search:

- **Limited inventory**—With search media, the inventory is fixed, like Super Bowl TV ads, the mailing list you are renting, or the readers of a low-circulation magazine. Only a certain number of people search for any keyword or phrase every day at the major search portals. This inventory shortage becomes even more of an issue, based on how most of the search media inventory is sold through auction-style, paid-placement distribution. So, if you want the media inventory (visibility and the resulting clicks), you need to pay the per-click rate that will result in the position you desire and deliver visitors (in the form of clicks to your website).

- **Inverse volume discounts**—A result of limited inventory and a real-time auction for position is a really crazy phenomenon where the more clicks and visibility (placement) you want, the more you pay on a per-click basis. The easiest way to illustrate this inverse volume discount is to start with a campaign, including a set of keywords and a particular overall spending level. Let's say that a $5,000 month-long test worked great—your Return on Investment (ROI) looks good with a CPO (Cost Per Order)/CPA (Cost Per Action), Return on Advertising Spend (ROAS), or branding metrics in line with expectations. Everyone is ecstatic. Now you want more: an increased budget to $20,000 a month. Unless you were at very low positions in the first instance on those keywords, that inventory may not even exist, and if it does, it's going to cost you more per click as you displace advertisers who currently occupy the positions above you that earn the search engines more revenue. Broadening your campaign to more keywords will help, but your list of relevant keywords is limited by your business sector. Make sure you are using every possible campaign permutation that you can get while keeping your conversion high. Although low-volume keywords help (when you add them up), the point of diminishing marginal returns can creep up on you.

> Make sure you are using every possible campaign permutation that you can get while keeping your conversion high.

- **Limited negotiation**—You can't negotiate in an auction. So you (or a search listings management company specializing in managing campaigns) will be adjusting listings within a marketplace that is nearly real-time, changing pricing and position. Because of the dynamic aspect of this marketplace, it is even more important that you have your objectives mapped out clearly. Although your objectives can be position, click volume, or Cost-Per-Click (CPC) averages/caps, a truly efficient campaign incorporates the post-click behavior differences into the ongoing campaign, focusing the campaign on keywords that work. If you want to exercise your negotiation skills, there are premium keyword placements available at most portals where reps do the deal making. Expect longer commitments when dealing with reps.

- **Unpredictable budget and click volume**—This is a biggie. How much should you allocate toward search if you have not done it before? Getting a fix on this is very difficult. You can get an approximate spend prediction for Yahoo!, Google, and Looksmart based on specific pricing, but these predictions assume predicted positions, Click-Through Rates (CTRs), CPCs, and click volumes. The Click-Through Rate has an impact on position and, therefore, on click volume (see Truth 10, "PPC search: CPM in disguise?"). Extensible Markup Language (XML) and directory-paid inclusion are even more difficult to predict. These feeds do not guarantee any position, and therefore no particular spend or traffic volume can be determined. Search campaign management companies can help you plan budgets in both XML and auctions, but often the best solution is to have a flexible budget based more on ROAS, or CPO/CPA.

3

- **Diverse conversion behaviors**—With search, as with other media, all clicks are not created equal. When optimizing by post-click behaviors, your individual keyword positions/prices need to go up or down based on post-click behaviors. For example, 40% of your initial spending may come from 20 high-volume keywords, but if half of these keywords exceed your post-click conversion cost objectives, you need to scale back those words (reduce positions) or eliminate them from the campaign altogether. Conversely, some keywords may be performing well, coming in under your CPO/CPA target. Look for opportunities to boost that kind of inventory. Also, remember, changes in position result in different conversion behaviors, because the network makeup changes within vendor distribution, and top positions often have more compulsive clickers.

- **Creative strategies**—I hope your copywriters don't mind working with some strange restrictions while also doing their best to balance call to action and prequalification copy across different formats. For example, Google allows 25, 35, 35 characters for title, description line 1, and description line 2 in its paid search listings, whereas Yahoo! is 40, 190. Editorial guidelines vary, like not using "click here" within Google, or no superlatives in Yahoo!. You might be able to do some prequalification or branding in your copy within Yahoo!, but in Google, your listing risks being demoted or deactivated for noncompelling copy that gets a poor CTR.

If you are not using SEM as part of your campaign, consider that it might be the most unobtrusive media out there. Internet searchers are online with a mission. Most media is interruptive and intrusive; search media facilitates the searcher's mission. The more you work with search engine media, the more you'll appreciate the power of this win-win scenario.

TRUTH

2

Intrusive media versus the psychic postal carrier

If your company buys advertising, most of it is very likely to be intrusive. In fact, many ad agencies pride themselves on the memorable and intrusive advertising they produce that "breaks through the clutter" of other advertising and catches consumers' attention. Direct response advertising such as direct mail intrudes on the activity of opening one's other mail, and infomercials are designed to capture the attention of the channel surfer. In order for all these types of advertising to effectively influence either branding metrics or eventual purchase, the ads must be seen and their messages understood.

Imagine how much more powerful direct mail advertising or catalog distribution could be if you could use a "psychic mailman" who waited outside the door of your best (or best potential) customers with hundreds of different messages and offers, and then rang the doorbell only at the moment your customer started thinking about researching or purchasing a specific product or expressing a particular need. When she thinks about a new down ski jacket, the psychic mailman tears out the appropriate page from your catalog and hands it over. The paid search (PPC) component of search engine marketing (SEM) can be your psychic mailman, delivering the perfect offers, at the perfect time, tuned to the specific needs being expressed by searchers.

> SEM can be your psychic mailman, delivering the perfect offer, at the perfect time....

The keywords

The foundation of a SEM campaign is the keyword list. The number of daily or monthly searches for every keyword in any campaign is finite. When a direct mail list performs, you wish an additional half a million names were available. Generally, additional identically converting names are not available, so you have to explore other lists that may share some similar characteristics with your winning list.

Paid placement search engine marketing has evolved into an auction marketplace in which you bid for keywords against your competitors in Google, Yahoo! (which may have been acquired by the time you read this), Microsoft's AdCenter, and other smaller search engines. If you don't bid high enough for keywords, your competition gets the higher position (visibility), the traffic, and the opportunity to gain a customer. It is critical that you have a system in place to determine the bid price that is appropriate, for every keyword, at every point in time, based on the conversion attributes of that keyword and your ROI objectives.

The creative

Just as a good rented direct mail list needs the right creative and offer, a good keyword list doesn't work in a vacuum. In SEM, you have two opportunities to tune creative. The first is the listing itself, which is like the cover of the catalog or envelope you provided to the psychic mailman. The first thing a searcher sees when he or she expresses a need by typing "cashmere sweater," "air purifier," or "Panasonic plasma HDTV" are the search listings that consist of a title (ranging in length from 25 characters to 40 or more characters) and a description (ranging in length from 70 to 190 characters).

Just as there are guidelines as to what is acceptable on the outside of an envelope, search ads are subject to certain editorial guidelines. Each ad's copy should be as compelling as possible to take advantage of the Click-Through Rate position bonus that Google in particular factors in when determining which ad position to award given a specific bid. The additional number of characters in Yahoo!'s auction environment allows for much more explanation of your offer, and a bit of prequalification might be appropriate. Test the effectiveness of your ad creative, just as you would different envelope designs. Unlike an envelope creative test, with SEM, you'll have your results very quickly—in as little as a week on a high-volume keyword.

An even more critical aspect of your creative is your site's landing page, where the searcher arrives after clicking on your ad. Think of your site's landing pages as the inside of your catalog or the letter mailed in the envelope delivered by your psychic mailman. Resist the temptation to use your home page as the landing page for your campaign. Don't hand the psychic mailman your regular catalog and force the customer to flip to the right page. Deposit the searcher on the best page, given the search terms they entered. Although you can't effectively test the costs of ten different catalogs, you can test ten landing pages with a modicum of effort, particularly if you engage the services of the right firm to manage your paid search marketing campaign.

Even if you don't have the resources to generate custom landing pages (so you can test lots of creative variables such as images, copy, price, and offers), chances are there are several existing landing pages on your site that might deliver dramatically improved conversions at no additional development cost to you. For example, which landing page on a tool catalog site will convert best for the search term "cordless drill," the home page, a search results page listing all the cordless drills with descriptions, a landing page listing only the top four best-selling drills, or the most popular drill product page modified to cross-sell to the alternative choices? Only testing will determine the answer.

Seasonality

Do you mail the same catalog all year round? If not, then empower your psychic mailman with tuned and updated keyword lists, ad creative, and landing pages, all tested and proven using the principles you live and breathe every day for all your direct marketing campaigns.

Testing, testing, testing

SEM provides you with an opportunity to implement a real-time feedback loop in which the campaign is adjusted based on the specific results of every keyword in every engine. You no longer have to accept the adage that "half of your ad budget is wasted." SEM, the psychic mailman, can not only eliminate the waste in your campaign, but also capitalize on opportunities.

As a seasoned direct and catalog marketer, you have a huge advantage in SEM. By adapting and applying the kinds of strategies that have worked for years to this relatively new medium, you can make a smooth transition into the world of SEM.

TRUTH

3

Search:
Beyond the
"new Yellow Pages"

Initially marketers thought of the search engines and advertising in search as a replacement for the *Yellow Pages* (either online or off). But search is much more than an online *Yellow Pages* substitute. There's a media revolution underway, and it will be powered by the search networks. Google has been testing the willingness of marketers to purchase newspaper, magazine, radio, and TV advertising, with Google acting as the broker, trafficker, and in the case of the test print ads, the production agency producing the layouts.

Would you buy additional advertising types from Google other than search? Chances are you already are. Google has a huge contextual network up and running on Blogger, Gmail, and thousands of sites, large and small, and you can buy both textual and graphical inventory in Google simply by opting in to have your ads placed more broadly. It seems like a major stretch for Google to jump from an online contextual advertising network to print advertising, but, in my opinion, that's the whole point of its tests: to determine how well the Google brand translates into other media.

One thing we already know is that Google is all about "doing the math"—they are very good at it, and getting better as they learn. The question is whether Google can execute a plan that truly allows it to become the portal through which advertisers buy a diversity of media, all in an auction format. The math required to run sophisticated multiplacement media auctions is nontrivial, but quite manageable. With automation and auctions come targeting, and advertising targeting

There's a media revolution underway, and it will be powered by the search networks.

is a great thing for both consumers and marketers. Marketers don't want to pay to reach those who are not in their target market, and consumers don't want to see advertising that is irrelevant to them. One can even argue that poorly targeted advertising (both online and offline) is one of the drivers of advertising burnout. For instance, I don't want to see a denture ad or a car ad, so exposure to it only serves to help me strengthen my advertising tune-out skills.

The search engine marketplaces have proved that valuable search media can be auctioned and result in a high price for valuable inventory, and these auction systems are being deployed for increasing amounts of online inventory. The most common online advertising to be auctioned in addition to search is the following:

- Channel-based text or banner placements

- Contextually targeted text or banner ads

- Behaviorally targeted inventory

Although the billing methods for the auctions may differ (including CPA, CPC, and CPM (Cost Per Thousand impressions, where M is the Roman numeral for thousands), the auction management systems have one thing in common: They are designed to maximize profit/yield to the publisher and the network. Network targeting and ad-serving systems, such as Google's AdSense, calculate in almost real-time the highest predicted yield among all the ads in a large database and then serve those ads.

In the future, I believe that valuable media assets other than online text and banners are likely to start showing up in the auction systems of the search players due to the following factors:

- The engines have a billing relationship with hundreds of thousands marketers.

- Major marketers using SEM are used to the uncertainty of an auction marketplace, even if they don't always like the ambiguity of delivery cost and visibility (position).

- Most of the search players have deep pockets, and if publishers are unwilling to release inventory on a revenue-sharing basis, the engines can either buy the inventory, or in a more extreme tactic, buy the media companies.

One can easily imagine a new world of media auctions, in which the search engine networks with the customer bases of active marketers and deep pockets might attack the major media markets. Following are some of the major media markets in addition to the Internet and search that might evolve to truly auction-based marketplaces. These spending estimates are based on reports by TNS Media Intelligence (http://www.tns-mi.com/newsIndex.htm):

- **Local and national newspapers (Ad spending: $26,007.20 million in 2007)**—Although it might take years before the majority of newspaper ad space is sold in an auction format, if auctions result in a higher net CPM to the publisher, that trend might accelerate. An added twist in the future is due to the digital printing revolution, where advertising can be segmented to different households by geography or demographics, as is currently done in search advertising.

- **Television, network, and spot (Ad spending: $38,020.10 million in 2007)**—Some television advertising is already sold in a rudimentary auction; the "TV Upfront" and Super Bowl spots are sold in an auction style. An auction for premium TV ad slots nationally and regionally could evolve where the advertiser that wants the audience the most gets the slot. Of course, this auction could run concurrently with auctions run within cable TV. IP addressable cable boxes could ensure that you and I never see an ad completely irrelevant to our households.

- **Cable TV (Ad spending: $17,842.20 million in 2007)**—Your cable company knows a lot about you and your family based on what your watch. TiVo knows just as much, maybe even more. They could deliver advertising on such a targeted basis that you might start liking advertising again.

- **Magazines (all types) (Ad spending: $30,327.50 million in 2007)**—Magazines, like newspapers, have some premium ad spaces such as inside front cover or front of the book. These could be auctioned across the full circulation or by geography. Again, digital printing could result in highly personalized magazine ad delivery (not to mention content delivery).

- **Radio (all types) (Ad spending: $10,691.70 million in 2007)**—Radio ad spots, like TV spots, are already produced and delivered in digital formats, and sales of remnant inventory are already auctioned using DMarc, a system purchased by Google.

Those of you who love offline media because costs are completely fixed in the annual media plan and insertion orders are locked in by January may have to rethink the way you buy media if the search engines have anything to say about it.

TRUTH

4

Search:
It's like the stock market

 The more you think about the stock market, commodities markets, and the auctions for search engine position, the more similarities you see. There are a limited number of shares of any stock, and in the commodities markets, there are fixed quantities of pork bellies or frozen concentrated orange juice. Buyers of stocks or commodities use internal information, external information, formulas, and gut instinct to bid within the marketplace. (Some even try to use insider information.) The reason buyers bid high is that they believe the true value of the stock or asset to be greater than the asking price in the marketplace.

Economists have a term that they apply to markets, marketplaces, and economic systems: friction. *Friction* relates to inefficiencies within a marketplace that result in mispricing of the assets being traded, bought, or sold in the market. The elimination of friction in a market brings a market closer to an efficient market. Much of the law on the books relating to the stock market regarding insider trading, disclosure of material information regarding publicly traded companies, and accuracy of accounting statements is based on maintaining an efficient, fair information flow. Similarly, commodities are sold in an open marketplace because sellers of those commodities feel that open marketplaces result in the highest prices for the commodities.

In the stock market, the scarcity of a company's publicly traded stock results in the price of that stock "clearing" at a point at which the perceptions of value of the buyers and the sellers are nearly exactly the same (or separated by a small bid-ask spread). The stock seller is convinced that in the long term or even short term, the price of the share of stock they already own will go down (or perhaps not grow sufficiently given the investor's goals). If the buyer wants more shares of a stock than there are sellers willing to sell at a given price, the buyer must increase the bid to encourage additional sellers to enter the market. When you are bidding on keywords within the search marketplaces of Google, Yahoo!, Microsoft, and the other search engines, you are using some rational (or possibly irrational) basis by which to make your decision. Traffic generated by each keyword or phase is a potential asset to the marketer, at the right price. Even the visibility of each listing being served may have a measurable branding value.

In SEM, it initially seems like the engines (Google, Yahoo!, and so on) are the sellers, and you compete with all your competitors on a keyword-by-keyword basis. But a more accurate way of viewing this situation is that you use the keyword position marketplaces to buy higher positions from your competition. While the engines are collecting your CPC fees, you are buying traffic, orders, and influence

> While the engines are collecting your CPC fees, you are buying traffic, orders, and influence away from your competitors.

away from your competitors. Competitors want each of their current positions, but if you've determined you want some of those positions (and the associated traffic) more than they do, you buy the position out from under them. Each position in Google or Yahoo! is really like its own stock with its own distinct value (to each marketer) and clearing price. So when the Google or Yahoo! rep gets you to raise your spending from $12,000 per month to $15,000 per month, that extra traffic is traffic you'll get that would have gone to one or more of your competitors. Similarly, when your listings get pushed down in the auctions, that's not the engine's doing—it is due to one of your competitors deciding that the traffic and visibility of your favorite keywords is worth more to them than it was to you. This holds the makings of a bid war, but only up to the values the marketers place on each position and keyword. Bidding wars (like emotional stock buying and selling) are destructive exercises that have no place in any sound investment strategy.

Even though we know better (notwithstanding some lunatics out there), let's hope that these bidding decisions in the marketplace are being made—whether manually or by campaign management software—based on rational business models. These business models might be simple ROI formulas or highly sophisticated valuation formulas that take immediate profit, multiple conversions, cross-selling, and lifetime value into account. Sometimes a bid will look to you like a ludicrous decision, whereas in fact there is a brilliant marketer working with a sophisticated software platform making very rational choices. The same situation happens in the stock market when we see price movements. Without knowing the other guy's data and formulas, we are stuck in the marketplace, making our own decisions based on our own data.

Some of the strategies, concepts, and rules that you would set for yourself when trading stocks should also hold true for buying search engine traffic, with one big difference. You have it within your power to create a reasonable estimate of each keyword listing's true value to you. This affords you a killer advantage, but only if you take the time to do the following:

- Know the market, learn from the experts, and apply best practices.

- Have a good idea of what your short-term and long-term objectives are.

- Know the factors driving your business profitability.

- Do research into the post-click behavior of each keyword listing.

- Understand that past data does not guarantee future results.

- Know the volatility in pricing for the keywords in your portfolio.

- Calculate the maximum price you can pay for traffic while still maximizing profits.

- Understand the tradeoff between click price and sales (or lead) volume (market elasticity).

Yes, this sounds like quite a lot of homework, but it will pay off when you enter the search engines' dynamic auction marketplaces. Applying quantitative and strategic processes and rapid decision automation to the search engine marketplace can be extremely profitable. But know what you are doing, because like the stock market, play it wrong and you can lose your shirt.

...know what you are doing, because like the stock market, play it wrong and you can lose your shirt.

TRUTH

5

Top organic position: It's not enough

One topic that continues to capture the attention of both in-house search engine marketers and those at agencies is the question of whether organic rankings can replace paid-placement rankings. Weaning oneself of PPC search listings when top organic listings have been achieved seems like a no-brainer. However, in this truth, I'll illustrate how pulling your PPC ads after achieving high organic position might, in fact, be a very bad idea.

Many SEO practitioners share a pitch that, with their help, you, the marketer, will be able to achieve top organic position for your favorite (or most valued) keywords and kick the PPC search habit forever. It sounds very tempting, and getting top organic positions does have a huge incremental value. This is particularly true if the page that ranks well contains a clear offer leading to a good conversion rate and site stickiness. So, knock

...pulling your PPC ads after achieving high organic position might, in fact, be a very bad idea.

yourself out and engage in SEO because (unless your landing pages are horrid and result in a high abandonment rate) you'll benefit from the visibility and "free" traffic that only costs you hours of work to achieve. However, you must remember that the ability to achieve top organic placement above any universal search elements is increasingly in doubt, except perhaps for a brand search.

Also consider that Search Engine Results Pages (SERPs) are no longer a "one size fits all" scenario. Personalized search will increasingly scramble the search results and, therefore, rank. Also, different syndication partners display listings differently. (Some even customize the algorithms for organic display.) So, you may feel like you've got high organic rank, whereas your true visibility is nowhere near as great.

Even if you were to apply the old-school mentality and assume that great SEO is consistent across all usage instances and decide to turn off PPC search for that keyword in those engines, you should consider the following issues:

■ **Competitive mix**—What is the mix of paid and organic listings? Are there competitors surrounding your paid and organic listings or the listings surrounding those of channel partners? If you are surrounded by enemies, gaining good PPC visibility will likely be more strategically important. Competitive mix analysis isn't a matter of black-and-white distinctions, because some of your channel partners may not be exclusive to you or may result in a lower immediate and lifetime profit than you'd realize by capturing the customer yourself. Don't get too scientific in this analysis because as we'll see, the decision may be a slam dunk either way.

> If you are surrounded by enemies, gaining good PPC visibility will likely be more strategically important.

■ **Messaging differences**—What is the messaging of your organic link? The organic title and description displayed are at least partially under your control, as is the copy on the landing page associated with the high-ranked listing. As you well know, messing with any on-page elements after achieving high rank is dangerous, so if the marketing messages on your organic pages are not conducive to converting visitors, you may need to rely on your paid-placement titles, descriptions, and landing pages to effectively communicate your message and offer to site visitors. Even if your organic listings have spot-on messaging and the landing pages are great, do you have more than one offer or more than one target audience? If the answer is affirmative, you will want to avail yourself of the flexibility that PPC listings offer.

■ **Conversion differences**—Here's where things get interesting. You have far more flexibility with ad copy and landing pages with PPC search than you do with organic, so consider the conversion rate differences during your analyses.

The preceding issues aside, the ultimate proof is in the test. To test the true value of the additional PPC listing, you need to determine the net additional costs and the net additional benefit or profit. The test my team uses is the "pulse test," which is structured as a one-week-on and one-week-off test wherein the PPC listings are paused. You'll want to keep a close watch on all your key post-click metrics for both organic and paid search.

Let's do the math

For most marketers, variables include conversion to lead/sale and (in the case of an e-commerce site), revenue/profit. Some lead-generation success metrics include scores (indicating the projected quality of the lead), so you may need to measure this, too:

1. If you are already running paid campaigns, use the results as your baseline, and if not, use the organic-only traffic, conversion, and revenue/profit/lead quality numbers as your baseline. Run the test for a full week and collect the data. If you are a smaller marketer and a week does not result in a statistically significant number of orders or leads, run the test for a couple of weeks or longer.

2. The next step is to switch states. Turn on/off the paid search listing and look at the delta in overall clicks, as well as the clicks from each source. The first calculation you'll want to make is the net click gain. You might find that there is some cannibalization wherein the paid listing takes clicks from your organic listing. But the net clicks delivered by the paid listing are used to calculate your true CPC. (That is, you want to add the cost of the cannibalized clicks to the net gain of clicks to determine true CPC.)

3. Finally, calculate the difference in total conversions and resulting revenue/profit/lead quality between both states. Pay particular attention to the differences between the organic and paid channels, as well as the net gain. You might find that paid search brings in a different, more valuable customer.

When I've tested this with clients, these calculations have always showed high ROI for the PPC campaign, even when cannibalization is factored in. The better the paid landing page, the higher the net gain in ROI. So far, I haven't found an instance where organic is enough. But I'll keep testing.

TRUTH

The rise of search

When the Internet first made its appearance as a mass phenomenon in the early 1990s, many pundits heralded its arrival by announcing that finally the era of "convergence" had arrived. Digital media would allow for the extension into cyberspace of existing empires in a way that reinforced old media power. Those who controlled both the content and the distribution of their assets would be the new leaders, and vast profits and synergies would be released in this grand convergence.

Although there was no such grand convergence, over time the content on the Internet did improve, broaden, and grow into millions of different niches—some of them fanciful, others purely pragmatic. Some of this content came from established media outlets and copyright owners, but a large share of it arose spontaneously from a vast, irregular army of independent publishers (some of whom published as a hobby without goals of earning a substantial revenue from advertising or subscriptions) and from e-commerce merchants who uploaded gigabytes of product information to the Web in order to better describe their offerings to shoppers or to provide online support to existing customers.

The quantity of information being uploaded to the Web and made accessible to the increasing throngs of visitors was growing exponentially, but it was a mass of poorly organized information of varying quality. Enter the search engines, categorizing and sorting through the increasing chaos and clutter. Because their sole purpose was to serve up these nearly infinite divergent channels in meaningful chunks to those who searched through them, the engines made a diverse field of information knowable, explorable, and (eventually) monetizable.

In retrospect, the phenomenal growth of search seems unsurprising because the function of search is so deeply ingrained in the human psyche. Before the first caveman crawled out of his cave, human beings have been searching for things to improve their lives. The urge to find, discover, and explore

...the engines made a diverse field of information knowable, explorable, and (eventually) monetizable.

is programmed into us, and it will continue for as long as we walk the planet. Searching, because it reflects a fundamentally human quest that is unconcerned with whatever form such information takes, be it text, images, graphics, sound files, or other yet-to-be-developed media form, is the most powerful, unifying activity ever formulated by digital media.

Search engines, in primitive form, had been available for many years—in fact, they predated the Web. As early as 1990, Archie, Veronica, and Gopher provided a fairly efficient way for people to get outside and rummage around the increasing torrent of (mostly academic) documents floating in cyberspace. They were then succeeded by the first generation of search engines specifically designed to index web pages: now-forgotten properties such as the World Wide Web Wanderer, Aliweb, WebCrawler, the World Wide Web Worm, and others.

In the Web's early days, web directories were more generally useful than these early search engines, and were the natural successors to link lists, which were simply web pages in which the publisher had embedded resources likely to be of interest to the site's readers. One such list called "Jerry and David's Guide to the World Wide Web" was launched in early 1994, and later became Yahoo!, the dominant directory on the Web today. Other popular general-subject directories included Excite, Lycos, and Magellen-McKinley, and they were accompanied by many specific-subject directories such as People Finders. Yahoo! survived because it was able to expand quickly from its humble directory roots through acquisitions, growing massively and doing everything possible to become what was then called a "sticky hub."

Unlike directories and portals, which were maintained by human editors, search engines were programs run by algorithms, and the first engines were both hard to use and produced highly erratic results. To use them effectively, it

...the first [search] engines were both hard to use and produced highly erratic results.

was necessary to bone up on Boolean logic and proximity operators (which looked for query terms existing within a user-specifiable character range in any web page), and even then it might produce seemingly endless pages of irrelevant results. One engine would only yield decent results by skillful use of the NEAR (proximity) operator. Another would gag on queries that weren't carefully formatted to adhere to its in-built case-sensitivities. Even the best engine with the largest index, AltaVista, had an annoying habit of spitting out results that were adulterated by long lists of clearly irrelevant queries. The experience was so exasperating that "how to search" books appeared, comparing the engines and recommending how users might best exploit them. For awhile, meta-search engines (which searched across multiple engines) provided more utility because they raised the odds that one of the engines would produce a relevant result. However, they were cumbersome to use, and with many queries, all they did was multiply the garbage that the engines were spewing out.

Goto.com, a search engine launched by serial entrepreneur Bill Gross in 1997, heralded the dawn of the Cost-Per-Click (CPC) advertising method. Charging advertisers by the click instead of the impression had been tried before in 1996 (by OpenText, LinkStar, and Yahoo!), but Goto.com's implementation of this method was the first widely successful instance of a CPC-based ad model. After users entered a query in the search box, they were exposed to a Search Engine Results Page (SERP) containing both "natural" search results compiled by the search engine, as well as text advertisements generated by the keyword. Goto.com established the basic model by which advertisers were able to gain visibility on SERPs. Keywords were sold in an electronic auction, and the marketer who paid the most would be rewarded with a placement at the top of the page, where the majority of clicks occurred. Marketers were billed not by impression, but by the click.

In the next truth, we learn how Goto.com led to Google, and how Google forever changed the lives of SEMs.

TRUTH

7

Goto.com and the birth of PPC search

Goto.com, launched in 1997, heralded the dawn of the CPC advertising method. Charging advertisers by the click instead of the impression had been tried before in 1996 (by OpenText, LinkStar, and Yahoo!), but Goto.com's implementation of this method was the first widely successful instance of a CPC-based ad model. After users entered a query, they were exposed to a SERP containing both "natural" search results compiled by the search engine, as well as text advertisements generated by the keyword. Goto.com established the basic model by which advertisers were able to gain visibility on SERPs. Keywords were sold in an electronic auction, and the marketer who paid the most would be rewarded with a placement at the top of the page, where the majority of clicks occurred. Marketers were billed not by impression, but by the click.

Many doubted that users would elect to click on these paid placements, but users did because, in many cases, these listings were exactly what they were looking for—especially if the nature of the query was commercial. In 1998, Goto's first year of operation, it booked about $800,000 in revenues. Four years later, it would book more than $600 million. Advertisers liked the way it worked, especially its self-serve console, which was simple, straightforward, and capable of providing a near real-time view of the effectiveness of a marketing campaign.

Goto's way of serving advertising represented a true revolution in the way advertising was thought of, consumed, and produced. Before Goto, advertising, including online advertising, was "attached" to a piece of content. This content might be an article, a web page, or a position on a high-traffic portal, but it was essentially a static element, like a billboard. Furthermore, given that only a small fraction of the viewers would ever act on its call to action, and even fewer would ever "convert"—or perform the action requested by the advertiser—this content-attached advertising was wasteful and inefficient. Search-based advertising, however, decoupled advertising's traditional attachment to content and was assembled dynamically and on-the-fly, answering to the actual intent of the user as evinced by the user's selection of keywords. This created a form of advertising that was as follows:

- Less wasteful because the advertiser no longer had to pay for impressions that were not likely to result in consumer action.

- More likely to be acted upon by the user because the ad was more relevant to what he or she had in mind.

- More profitable to publishers, given that they could now offer traffic that, differentiated by a search engine, could be matched to multiple advertisers willing to pay much more for it than for undifferentiated traffic.

In effect, Goto, not Google, was the real inventor of this revolutionary way of serving advertising, and the story behind how Goto failed to capitalize on this innovation is a complicated and somewhat tragic story. Suffice it to say that Goto.com was always dependant on Microsoft and Yahoo! to serve the traffic it needed to monetize its site, whereas Google already had the traffic. Once Google had cloned Goto's technology to serve up paid results along with its organic results, it was able to turn itself into a cash machine.

Google was first and foremost a search engine, and its major innovation was the addition of PageRank, a popularity-ranking factor. PageRank took account of the number and quality of incoming links to any given web page or site in order to determine its objective merit. PageRank, when factored in with other elements of a given web page that indicate relevance, produced search results that were astonishingly pertinent, almost as if they had been evaluated by a very wise and careful human. Google's relevancy engine (which now includes many additional relevancy-weighing factors) was so much better than those offered by competing engines that it quickly became the preferred search engine among many web users. It also attracted the attention of several large portals, including AOL/ Netscape, a development that caused Google's query traffic to grow beyond 3 million searches per day.

> ...it [Google] was able to turn itself into a cash machine.

Google's founders were aware of Goto.com, but until 2001 believed that the addition of paid search results would alienate Google's growing flock of users. Rejecting a partnership offer from Goto, they launched AdWords, a web-based, self-service ad platform that worked very similarly to Goto by allowing marketers to quickly compose text ads, bid on keywords, and enter the advertising business for just $5.00. Over the next two years, Google expanded its distribution greatly, including to portal powerhouse AOL, whose 34 million members vastly increased the reach of marketers using AdWords. In 2003, to maximize the distribution possibilities for AdWords-placed CPC ads, Google launched a contextual advertising product and soon thereafter acquired Applied Semantics. Google technology was integrated into Applied Semantic's AdSense, a program that enabled web publishers to monetize their site traffic through the display of contextually targeted ads. AdSense became a huge incremental revenue source for Google, thereby extending its money-making reach beyond search. This allowed Google, through partnerships with website owners, to begin monetizing the remaining time a user spent online.

In effect, advertising-supported search engines eliminated three traditional barriers to electronic media advertising, which had existed since its inception. The first was the threshold amount of money that marketers needed to have on hand to be advertisers. Even tiny marketers who had never seriously thought of doing digital marketing could afford the modest $5.00 entry fee. The second was the traffic thresholds required by the big online ad networks in order to run advertising on web pages, which allowed small web publishers to include advertising on their sites.

Lastly, Google and Goto changed advertising from what had traditionally been the domain of the agencies, specialists, media buyers, and broadcasters, and made advertising available to everyone.

TRUTH

8

Google introduces
relevance and yield

Google launched its AdWords paid-placement advertising service in 2000 and has been making continual improvements to it since that time. Although the CPCs in search advertising were initially low, they've risen both as the number of paid search advertisers has increased, and Google and the other engines have improved the relevance of these ads, making them worth more to advertisers.

AdWords has come a long way in just a few years. When it launched, its operation was very similar to that of Goto.com: a straight auction in which position on the SERP was influenced directly by the amount that any advertiser would pay to secure such a position. But as Google grew, became a public company, and sought to maximize the amount of money it could charge for paid listings, it began to tinker with AdWords by adding additional factors to its system in order to better predict a given ad's relevance and charge accordingly.

One of the most significant changes to AdWords has been Google's incorporation of a mechanism called Quality Score. Many search marketers, including some on Google's staff, often appear to demonstrate an incomplete understanding of the specifics of what makes up the Quality Score. Although Google provides some guidance on its blog (http://adwords.blogspot.com/), I've found that the information from Google isn't always in one place nor is it always clear about the cause and effect that campaign structure, ad relevance, keyword relevance, and starting position have on the Quality Score over time.

> Many search marketers, including some on Google's staff, don't really understand the specifics of what makes up the Quality Score.

Generally, the easiest, most effective way to think of Google's Quality Score is as a system that analyzes predicted CTR (normalized for position), and also factors in variables relating to post-click relevance. For example, Google collects CTR data for your ad regardless of your position and compares it against the norms for that position and possibly the norms within the SERP for that specific search query (that is, your neighboring competition). By normalizing the data (factoring in your position), Google is attempting to evaluate ads on a level playing field.

It shouldn't matter, then, if your ad is in position one or six; your Quality Score will still be calculated accurately. However, after reviewing tens of thousands of ad groups and millions of keywords, I've found that one listing often gets a bit of a boost in Quality Score when it runs in the top-three SERP positions because data is collected much more quickly in top positions, and the normalization curve may not be perfectly accurate. This positive effect might only be temporary and might only hold for as long as Google gathers more data on your ads and the competing ads around you.

Consequently, you might blow your ROI by aggressively bidding for keywords after the launch of a new AdGroup or campaign in the hopes that a good Quality Score will help you in the long run. For this reason, many search practitioners recommend an aggressive start to a campaign, both to learn Quality Score quickly and to take advantage of any inherent bias in the Google algorithm with respect to assigning an artificially high Quality Score to higher positioned ads.

In a nutshell, then, anything you can do to increase your predicted CTR, regardless of which position you happen to obtain, is a good thing. Google is continually refining the way that Quality Score works and made several significant refinements in 2008. With the new changes to its Quality Score calculation, Google states "Quality Score is now more accurate— because it is calculated at the time of each search query."

...anything you can do to increase your predicted CTR, regardless of which position you happen to obtain, is a good thing.

This can be interpreted in many ways, but in the very brief time that this change has been live, it looks like Google has given itself more flexibility in terms of calculating Quality Score in real time for broad matches, as well as for adjusting Quality Score based on other factors that may correlate with predicted CTR. Many of those factors might never be disclosed by Google, but I've seen enough variation in ad CTRs, based on a wide variety of variables above and beyond position, that we can imagine that day-part, geography, or even IP address block (ISP) are now being used as potential adjusting factors to your real-time Quality Score.

It will come as no surprise that these changes will likely result in higher Google spending at the same time as relevance of the search result increases. Google gets better at picking the relevant ads with the higher click-through rate (CTR) while the bids and billed CPCs rise simultaneously.

TRUTH

9

The rise of content and context

Normal online contextual advertising targeting matches the ad being shown to the editorial content on the page or site in which it appears. The better the ad is targeted to this content, the happier are both the marketer and surfer.

Both marketers and surfers prefer a well-targeted ad, as do the publishers. The publisher knows that generally, the better targeted the advertisement is, the more he can charge for it (directly or through an ad network). Although the extremely high level of targeting generated by a well-tuned contextual network is highly desirable, the results still might not measure up to pure search targeting for some marketers or campaign segments. Targeting alone does not always translate into the same surfer mindset as pure search. As Danny Sullivan has pointed out, there is a difference between "search mode" and "surf mode." Therein lies the core of the quality issue. Does it make a difference for you?

For some marketers, the quality (conversion rate as a percentage of visitors) for content-driven clicks is lower than the remainder of pure search inventory. Other marketers have not seen a difference in conversion quality. For example, Chris Seahorn, Director of Business Development at eBags, notes, "I have not seen a drop in conversion quality within my Google AdWords campaigns." However, after a bit more digging, we uncovered the fact that Chris does not yet have a very high level of content inventory mixed in with the pure search inventory. Other marketers are currently enthusiastic but are reserving final judgment. John Rogers, Director of E-Commerce Marketing at Orvis (a well-respected and well-known catalog marketing company), says, "we monitor the conversion and quality of our traffic on an ongoing basis and have not seen any change in quality; however, we will be watching the conversion quality carefully."

To test how well content inventory works for you, you might need to enlist the help of a technologically savvy search marketing professional, and/or enlist the help of your webmaster. Currently, the only way to identify the source of the paid search traffic delivered from both Google and Yahoo! is through the Hypertext Transfer Protocol (HTTP) referrer. The HTTP referrer is stored by a browser and supplied to the server and works in the following manner:

1. A visitor who is on the way to your site clicks on a link (paid or unpaid, search or contextual).

2. The visitor's browser stores the referring site information in a referrer field.

3. This information is normally relayed to your server in the header of the request for your landing page. (After all, the browser needs to request a page from your server to display it to the surfer.)

4. By looking at the referrer data, you can usually determine if the search originated through a context/content or pure search link.

However, the referrer is not reported by all browser versions and is stripped out by some firewall software. Also, if you run your clicks through an ad server, this ad server may strip out the referrer, making it difficult to run such an analysis (unless you have the ability to tap referrer data and run conversion analysis at the ad server level). Google referrers are easy to identify, because each one contains a common element that can be identified (for example, googlesyndication.com). Currently, Yahoo! has no such network-wide content click-through identifier. Assuming you already have your inbound Yahoo! links tagged uniquely, a highly sophisticated tech team could create a complex filter that looks for Yahoo! link-tagged referrers missing search term queries. The referrer that matches with the Yahoo! inbound tag, but is missing a search query string, can be assumed to have originated from a context/content listing, or a list of the content sites can be matched against the inbound traffic.

Because none of the major search networks append landing page URLs (Uniform Resource Locators) with a content source tag (which means you lose some referrer data), you can't tell every visitor's

...making the right opt-in or opt-out decision becomes critical.

origination type with complete certainty. Of course, some data is better than no data, and as the percentage of content inventory goes up, making the right opt-in or opt-out decision becomes critical.

If the content inventory works for you at the price you are paying, you certainly won't want to miss out on that traffic and give the click to your competition. On the other hand, if the segment of your budget being spent on the content-based portion of your campaign is not meeting your objectives at the CPC you have to pay, you will be foolish not to reallocate that budget elsewhere (perhaps to new keywords or to improving the efficiency of your existing campaign).

To get the most of your content ads, make sure the creative/offer in the ad is well tuned simultaneously for searchers and surfers, because each group is likely in a completely different mindset. Remember to write creative appropriately when opted into content advertising. The difference in conversion behavior between those in "surf mode" and "search mode" may be much less for broad terms. Someone searching for "music" or someone visiting a music site with content match links could be in a similar state of mind. However, someone who types in "music download" in a search box may be more inclined to take action than a surfer reading an article on music downloads clicking on an ad out of curiosity. On the other hand, if the ad and offer are compelling, there may be no difference in quality. For an example of successful content targeting, our conversion experience with Google has been good for ads running on articles about Google's AdSense at associateprograms.com, the Google weblog, and traffick.com. The contextual match provided by the Google AdSense system in all these cases is quite good. We also have several clients for whom buying content inventory in both Yahoo! and Google has been quite successful.

If you use Yahoo! or Google, it won't be long before the floodgates open and inundate you with content-based traffic. You'd better know if you want this traffic or not. The best way to decide is to start thinking about a testing and decision process now.

You'd better know if you want this traffic or not....

TRUTH

10

PPC search:
CPM in disguise?

As online marketers, we all purchase advertising based on some form of CPM, CPC, or CPA. Generally, marketers prefer to pay for performance and, therefore, are drawn to CPA or CPC forms of advertising, where the consumer has already chosen to interact or transact with the ad, website, or message before the advertiser needs to pay.

Google, Yahoo!, and Microsoft continue to be an important source of visibility, visitors, revenue (or leads), and profit for search engine marketers and businesses in general. The search engines' large reach and their CPC performance-based pricing model have resulted in a dramatic shift of budgets from other media into PPC search. The thinking is that CPC pricing provides the marketer with a "free ride" when it comes to visibility in the search results and free branding for those searchers who see an ad but don't click. However, you should be aware that just like any other media, the search engines are constantly striking a balance between serving your needs as a marketer, the needs of searchers and, of course, revenue maximization for themselves and their syndication partners. After all, the search engines are in business to maximize both short-term and long-term revenue and profitability, and we, as marketers, are the source of that revenue; the audience of searchers is the asset we want access to. So, we need to understand that this revenue imperative at the search engines means that over time, we have to work harder to get the results we want from paid listings.

> ...over time, we have to work harder to get the results we want from paid listings.

Even though the search engine media invoice you pay is based on CPCs, the reality is that the search engines are actually running their keyword visibility auctions based almost entirely on eCPM (effective Cost Per Thousand Impressions...C is used because it is the roman numeral for thousand) and eRPS (effective Revenue Per Search). Because the search engines are, in essence, packaging up CPM advertising in a CPC layer, it is critical that marketers understand the algorithmic basis for these decisions.

Here's how the revenue-maximizing algorithm for all the search engines works. The search engine ad display system selects and displays ads in the order of the effective CPM of each ad, against the specific search query and the other information the engine has about the searcher, rather than in order of the maximum specified CPCs. It's not just a matter of what one advertiser is bidding versus another advertiser. This means the ads with the highest effective CPM are placed in heaviest rotation, maximizing revenue. For example, an ad with a 4% click-through and a $.25 CPC ($10 CPM) rotates into higher positions than an ad with a $.35 CPC and a 2% click-through ($7 CPM). The higher CPC does not get better placement. Google's CPM-based revenue maximization system might have been a factor in the recent AOL and Ask Jeeves deals, where those search engines realized they could not match the same revenue per search as Google could. At press time for this book, a similar scenario is playing out with Yahoo!, which is realizing that Google's algorithm is better at selecting the ads most likely to get clicked and, therefore, earn the most money per search.

To succeed in Google, Yahoo!, and Microsoft, you must run your campaigns using CPM-like strategies, with copy and keywords selected for high relevance and CTRs. If any marketer selects poor keywords or attempts to prequalify a searcher in Google, the ad will fall out of rotation and possibly be deactivated altogether, due to poor CTR, based on the impressions where the ad has been served. Ads that get higher CTRs relative to their neighboring competitors' ads will be able to achieve more at lower bids and will, therefore, get better position and rotation.

It sometimes makes sense to prequalify clickers by eliminating those who might not be a good fit through the fine-tuning of ad copy. However, any attempt to eliminate some consumers from clicking on your ad results in a low predicted CTR, and you'll have to bid much more to achieve the same position, due to the revenue-maximizing algorithm. The search engines have a large opportunity cost when searchers skip ads, so they have balanced that by forcing low-performing advertisers to pay more.

To thrive in the new search engine marketing environment, where CPC is looking a lot like CPM advertising, marketers must do the following:

- Select the right keywords and phrases to test and manage in a campaign. These keywords resonate with the brand and the content on the advertiser site.

- Write ad copy that balances call to action with education/pre-qualification to keep click-throughs at reasonable levels. All the search engines allow for simultaneous testing of ad copy, so there is no excuse not to test a variety of ads.

- Have landing pages (where the searcher lands after clicking) that convert those searchers to revenue effectively. Test variations and offers because not only does this make you the most money, but also the leverage of the higher conversion rate is leverage to be used when setting bids.

- Manage the campaign in an automated manner, based on measured conversion, to optimize the campaign. Use a specialized vendor, or if the campaign is small, manage it manually.

- Use the measurement and metrics data for site-related decisions (that is, pricing, call-to-action copy, product mix).

Google, Yahoo!, and Microsoft use analytics, technology, and strategy to maximize their revenue. Advertisers can do this, too. By applying metrics in an automated and intelligent way, advertisers can manage campaigns strategically, based on CPA, CPO, ROAS, or ROI, not based on emotion. The search engines have a responsibility to maximize their CPM revenue to meet their obligations to shareholders—that is the opposite of your objective, which is to get the most profit out of a media opportunity as possible. Don't be lulled into a false sense of security because you are buying the search advertising on a "performance basis."

> Don't be lulled into a false sense of security because you are buying the search advertising on a "performance basis."

TRUTH

11

The search tax:
Are search engines
leeches?

I hear an undercurrent of discontent from more and more marketers these days. Increasingly, they're concerned that search engines and pay-for-performance marketing channels (such as affiliate marketing) have turned into tolls. The claim is that these advertising and sales channels are becoming less about customer acquisition and more about paying—repeatedly—to maintain share of wallet with existing customers.

The online marketing ecosystem has evolved in an interesting way, creating unexpected pinch-points or conduits through which customers generally pass by choice (even if they don't have to). Search engine SERPs and organic landing pages generated by affiliates well-versed in SEO represent a huge segment of inbound traffic to marketers. They have the canceled checks to prove it.

At first glance, it seems that search engines and affiliates are often in positions to get a free ride, making money by capitalizing on the interest stimulated through a merchant's or brand holder's advertising, marketing, PR, and even sales efforts. Consequently, many might call the search engines and affiliate marketers leeches. After all, a big segment of customers originating through these channels are existing customers, returning with a price tag attached.

Affiliates often use both paid and organic search results to generate revenues, leveraging the content and brand-names obtained from the merchants. Are the search engines any different when they sell clicks from the query demand generated through a marketer's advertising, PR, and buzz? Do the engines unfairly appropriate and leverage the copyrighted material on billions of websites, and then charge for clicks from humans who already know they want to access a merchant or content site? Do affiliates who use PPC arbitrage or create organic pages that rank highly for brands, trademarks, and model numbers unfairly profit, joining the search engines by sucking the profit out of the marketers' and merchants' pockets without adding value?

The answers clearly depend on your perspective. But the alternative to paying the continued fees to both affiliate and search engines might be even more painful than the ongoing toll marketers pay to gain (and regain) customers through search and affiliate channels. Consumers are changing their behavior, and forward-thinking marketers need to reach them where they live, which is increasingly in the online space. To continue capturing these customers, marketers are necessarily tied to the new ecosystem. To gain some perspective on this issue, let's take a step back, looking at the world of advertising, marketing, and sales outside the Internet.

Consumers are changing their behavior, and forward-thinking marketers need to reach them where they live....

Advertising and marketing aren't just about getting new customers; they're also about holding onto the customers you already have and maximizing share of wallet for customers you might share with your competition. Coke and Pepsi have, at this point, had nearly every cola drinker as a customer at least once. Yet the two organizations continue to spend hundreds of millions of dollars on advertising, sponsorships (think *American Idol*), and in-store promotions (including slotting fees). The costs associated with airlines' frequent flyer programs are designed to stimulate loyalty as well.

The truth is that a healthy chunk of revenues for the vast majority of companies are funneled toward marketing to maintain share of wallet and customer loyalty. This practice is long-standing and established in the offline media world, and yet for some reason the Internet is judged by a completely different set of standards. It's easy to accuse Google, Yahoo!, Microsoft, and the affiliate networks of being leeches because they're so visible in the value chain, and because their value seems invisible. Consumers have simply changed their behavior from watching TV and reading newspapers to surfing and searching. TV networks and newspapers that don't have strong online migration plans will suffer as the consumers' eyeballs migrate online.

What's difficult for marketers to swallow, however, is the clear evidence that the search engines (and affiliate marketers with good organic rank on brand terms) have the power to insert themselves between the consumer and the brand, even when consumers clearly have an interest in the brand (as indicated by their search query containing the brand or trademark). Some (including American

...it does seem unfair that marketers who've spent millions or billions over the years to establish brand equity must now repurchase their own branded terms....

Airlines) have even resorted to lawsuits against the search engines in an attempt to enjoin competitors from bidding on their brand keywords; so far, these efforts have all been unsuccessful, either failing in court or being settled out of court.

Yes, it does seem unfair that marketers who've spent millions or billions over the years to establish brand equity must now repurchase their own branded terms, and it's understandable that many might be tempted to refuse to pay for brand keywords, sticking instead to the generic keywords that are clearly aimed at any given target audience. But in every case we've tested (and I have tested many and will likely test many more), doing so would be a mistake, even when the marketer has high organic rank on his brand. The results of every test we've executed indicate that the incremental gain received when paying for traffic on a brand term has a very high net ROI because

- Significant additional screen real estate on the SERP is gained.

- The total control over title and description allows for greater offer control.

- Top positions on one's brand usually aren't very expensive due to the engines' relevance algorithms.

- The ability to control and tune the landing page results in a conversion rate percentage, which in many cases is higher for the combined pages than for one alone.

I urge you not to think of Google and its brethren as leeches any more than other media are leeches. Think of search as the net you cast to capture the demand created by all your sales, marketing, PR, and advertising efforts. Fail to cast this net, and your customers will get away. Perhaps a more productive way to think about all these costs is to regard them as Customer Relations Management (CRM) expenditures.

TRUTH

12

Search versus keyword-targeted versus behavioral

When advertisers have difficulty extracting more volume from search, either due to lack of inventory or CPC prices that are difficult to justify, it might be time to take a closer look at quasi-search media, such as contextual or behavioral, to determine if these search-like media deliver on campaign objectives, and whether these objectives are branding, direct response, or a hybrid of the two.

Over the last several years, the lines between what marketers have traditionally defined as search and other targeting methods have blurred, for better or worse. However, even if the definitions of PPC search are blurring, particularly among less-sophisticated marketers, as search marketing professionals, we need to understand the differences between "pure search" and other targeting methods. Overall campaign efficiency may depend on our understanding of the flavors of quasi-search and how they fit into an integrated campaign that may include other online and offline media.

When I ask marketers if they consider keyword-targeted, text-based contextual advertising to be part of their search budget, they almost always say that it is. The same holds true for behavioral search retargeting, at least when such retargeting is accomplished with text links. When I ask about display advertising that is contextually or behaviorally targeted, the answers become more mixed. Some marketers still see any keyword-targeted media as search, but drawing the line is no longer as easy.

Many behavioral targeting systems use search as a trigger to group all searchers within a single category in order to make it easier to buy this traffic in bulk. Cynics might claim that the decision to remove targeting precision in exchange for volume is done primarily to appease media buyers willing to trade precision for scale. As sophisticated search buyers, however, we must continue to preach the benefits of increasing relevance and control and continue to request that engines and media providers give us access to tools that allow precise control over the level of targeting. Doing so is

> Some marketers still see any keyword-targeted media as search, but drawing the line is no longer as easy.

essential so that we can make intelligent decisions about how to spend budgets that might be thought of as search but are, in fact, becoming more of an integrated media purchase.

SEM and interactive agencies with strong skill sets in search (or even in-house teams that are extremely search savvy) are uniquely positioned to tap the incremental media opportunities whose targeting is based on keywords, regardless of whether the targeting methods are contextual or behavioral.

My recommendation with respect to the time when marketers should start exploring the behavioral and contextual media opportunities are when one or more of the following is true:

■ Marketers have found it difficult to extract more value from "pure search," even after going through several performance-enhancing iterations of expansion and segmentation.

■ They are in a highly competitive category.

■ Although their primary focus is on direct response, they are also building awareness and want to influence consumers toward their brand.

■ They have high levels of combined organic and paid search traffic (which can be utilized for retargeting the site's existing search traffic).

■ They have an agency or technology capable of monitoring the interaction effects between "pure search" and the quasi-search media of behavioral and contextual.

■ Their agency or technology can optimize the contextual or behavioral buys in conjunction with the search buy to assure that interaction effects are properly accounted for.

At a recent Search Engine Strategies conference held in San Jose, I had the privilege of joining several speakers on a panel dedicated to the exploration of opportunities within behavioral search retargeting. The common theme included optimism with respect to the size of the behavioral search retargeting market, as well as demonstrations of how improved targeting based on behavioral search resulted in improved relevance for the consumer over broader contextual or channel-based targeting methods, while simultaneously delivering

...a correctly implemented behavioral search retargeting can significantly enhance conversion rates.

targeting benefits to the advertiser. Optimism about behavioral search retargeting is warranted, because a correctly implemented behavioral search retargeting can significantly enhance conversion rates. The degree of conversion rate lift depends on many external factors, including the time interval between searching and buying for any given vertical. For example, the time interval between searching and buying is vastly different for car buyers than it is for consumers of consumer electronics or downloadable files.

As the search engines, publishers, and third-party networks roll out more sophisticated contextual and behavioral media options that are keyword-driven, budgets increasingly flow into anything that marketers consider search. As mentioned previously, most marketers consider both contextual and behavioral retargeting of search to be within "search budgets." In my view, SEM agencies and the skill sets that SEM agencies provide will be increasingly necessary to manage tomorrow's increasingly complex, quantitatively driven online media plan. Evidence of this fact exists in the continuing acquisitions of SEM firms by general interactive advertising agencies and ad holding companies. Traditional advertising agencies are waking up to the fact that they must significantly upgrade their technological processes and infrastructure to master the new generation of targeting methods, or their clients will quickly abandon them.

Regardless of where the line eventually ends up being drawn between search media and other media whose targeting is based on keywords, concepts, or behavior, the skills, strategies, and best practices we learn in PPC search campaign management will be highly valuable over the next several years. Even in the midst of the current economic turmoil, which has reduced many marketers' willingness to spend freely on untargeted media, the future looks bright.

TRUTH

13

Competitive and network click fraud: Problems and solutions

There's a crisis brewing in this wonderful industry, and it has the potential to hit marketers hard while also negatively impacting the search engines. The problem can be described generically as *click quality*, which manifests itself in many ways. Network click fraud, competitive click fraud, and mislabeled traffic are some of the culprits. These problems drive down the value of a click stream and, therefore, force marketers (if acting rationally) to lower bids or remove themselves from the marketplace completely. Impression fraud places the "wrong" listings higher in engines that count click-through rate (CTR) against impressions as part of a ranking algorithm (as with the Google's AdWords system).

I'll cover each of these cancers on the industry and explain how they hurt almost everyone except the "cheaters," who are unfairly benefiting.

Network click fraud

Network click fraud occurs when a syndication partner (a smaller publisher or search engine), receiving and displaying paid placement or contextual results from a search network, engages in the manufacturing, creation, or misrepresentation of clicks being delivered to its network partner.

When a network partner manufactures clicks-throughs using human or robotic means, this traffic is of vastly lower quality than that produced by humans looking for information to solve a problem. The addition of this useless traffic to the network might seem initially to benefit the network owner (often a search engine itself). After all, the network owner shares click revenue with the publisher. However, the network owner also has to worry about network quality. Most marketers, particularly the biggest spenders, measure their traffic quality and make campaign mix and bid changes based on empirical conversion or other quality measurement data. As the volume of sub-par traffic in a network increases for any specific market segment, the click prices drop, and the remaining publishers in the network get hurt. Actually, the capability of a network to get deals renewed with quality publishers requires that they not accept members to the network that will dilute network click quality. Google Chief Financial Officer George Reyes was probably focusing on the network type of click fraud when he said at an investor conference, "I think something has to be done about this really, really quickly, because I think, potentially, it threatens our business model."

Competitive click fraud

Competitive click fraud is a big problem for smaller businesses, particularly when the service provided is of great value (or great lifetime value), resulting in high CPCs. Lawyers, doctors, accountants, IT consultants, and, of course, SEM/SEO firms all bid in a marketplace with high CPCs. The higher the CPCs, the more affect a competitor can have on a specific budget. Terms such as "New York Lawyer" are currently at CPC costs in excess of $10. A click a day from five people from a competitor on a listing in each of the two major engines, and you are looking at an extra $1,500 a month on each of Google's and Yahoo!'s bills. $3,000 a month is a serious additional cost when that cost has no potential for benefit.

I've seen log entries in our server logs from competitors that have come through paid links and returned more than once. Was it click fraud or natural curiosity by a competitor who was considering working in our agency program? I'll never know for sure. What I do know is that SEO-related keyword clicks are not cheap. The competitive nature of business sometimes involves a high level of personal emotional dislike between the major players, which can result in a temptation to engage in click fraud. Resist the temptation, and do unto others....

Can you catch competitive click fraud? Perhaps you can—it depends on the level of sophistication of your competitor. IP address lookups are the most common method of identification of click fraud, combined with cookie tracking, session tracking, and normalized benchmarking. However, smaller businesses are likely to use Internet connections that don't directly identify them.

> The competitive nature of business sometimes involves a high level of personal emotional dislike between the major players....

Impression fraud

Impression fraud is the newest threat to the marketer. Google and other engines rely on an AdRank method of determining relevance of an ad. Imagine a competitor pausing his campaign while a sudden fraudulent or faked surge in impressions on your keywords was to occur—all these impressions would occur with ZERO clicks. Competing ads, including yours, would see their AdRank scores drop through the floor. Then the single, evil competitor waits a little while and then swoops in with a nice, normal ad with high CTR. Your campaign is entrenched with keywords disabled or seriously crippled.

Correctly labeling traffic

No doubt Google, Yahoo!, Microsoft, Ask, and the other search engines have learned more about both advertiser perception of the click fraud issue and the confusion in the marketplace brought about by lawsuits and an explosion of companies offering pure click fraud monitoring solutions. The crux of the click fraud issue is that marketers should not have to pay for clicks that are not authentic or valid. A tangential issue is not only what a fraudulent click is, but also what other clicks might not be suitable as media and, therefore, should not be charged to the SEM. The goal would seem to be to define and determine what is a "billable click." Even if we can achieve a black-and-white definition of a click and a billable click, we are left with the challenge of measuring and validating clicks.

Impression fraud and the fuzziness in the way impressions are (were) sometimes counted nearly derailed the online advertising business in its first decade. Similarly, click quality and click measurement standards are required to make sure that all parties engaged in SEM are on the same page (pun intended). In the end, search traffic and the success of search engine marketers, search engines, and even the industry as a whole depends on correctly labeled traffic coming from higher-quality network partners (or inexpensive, lower-quality networks).

> Competitive click fraud is a big problem for smaller businesses....

TRUTH

14

Better targeting with Microsoft adCenter

As marketers begin to truly understand the value impressions and clicks bring to their businesses, they will bid more for the opportunity. The pressure to fight for scale (click or impression volume) within auctions can be grueling. For those with strong businesses, strong brands, and compelling offers, auction-based media offer great opportunities.

PPC search entered a new era with the launch of Microsoft's adCenter (adcenter.microsoft.com), which launched in 2006 after a long beta period. As is common in SEM, the industry continually evolves to better meet the needs of all constituents. In addition to having another PPC auction to participate in, the advent of adCenter means that marketers are being offered a higher level of targeting than ever.

With more accurate targeting, this industry can move one step closer to a perfect marketplace; one in which people see only ads relevant to them, and preferably at a time when that ad is most relevant. When marketers can better target ads, they'll pay higher prices for advertising. This has been a primary driver of increased CPC in the PPC ad markets.

> With more accurate targeting, this industry can move one step closer to a perfect marketplace....

Like Google's AdWords and Yahoo!'s YSM (Yahoo! Search Marketing), Microsoft's adCenter runs its own PPC auction in which marketers bid for position on SERPs. Unlike Google and Yahoo!, which both have content networks, adCenter's ad serving is currently restricted to Microsoft-owned search properties. Another feature distinguishing adCenter from its rivals is the fact that it was the first service to let advertisers incorporate demographic data into the keyword-buying process. This data is derived from registration information from Hotmail, a web-based e-mail service with some 260 million users worldwide. Users of Hotmail must disclose information including name, gender, birth year, country/region, state, and zip code; although this information isn't guaranteed to be accurate, the assumption is that most users enter truthful data.

adCenter lets you select your audience segments with great precision. Would you like to target women 18–25 with your advertising, because they're more likely to buy your product or they're the kind of profitable customers you dream of? If women or men of any age are a high-value segment within your overall target audience, you can boost your bid per click on any keyword for that segment alone.

adCenter provides a whole new level of targeting by allowing marketers to better select their target audience by age, gender, geography, or day-part (time of day or day of week). Once you have an adCenter account, you'll learn more about keyword searchers by demographic than you ever knew (unless you subscribed to some expensive research panel services). Do a keyword lookup in adCenter, and you're presented with keyword counts and a breakdown of these totals by the following:

■ **Age** (five demographic segments: 18–25, 25–35, 35–50, 50–65, and 65+). Although it seems some ages belong to more than one bucket, this might just be a labeling issue. Also, even though there could be a 13–18 category under U.S. law, MSN has chosen not to offer it at this time.

■ **Gender**. Male/Female.

■ **Geography** (designated marketing areas, or DMAs).

■ **Wealth** (available for the U.S. market only). Wealth categories include Upper Elite, Lower Elite, Upper Affluent, Upper Middle, Lower Middle, and Bottom Third. This data is derived from the user's zip code entry, which, according to common industry practice, is used to derive inferences about a given user's economic profile.

■ **Lifestyle** (determined by multiple data points derived from MSN's multiple online properties, including MSN and Hotmail). Lifestyle subcategories include Prosperous Middle Income, Prosperous Family, Young Singles, White Collar Middle Income, Prosperous Retired, Blue Collar Middle Income, Lower Income Family, Urban Lower Income, and Rural).

These data, and deeper information, may affect keyword selection—and not just for Microsoft's engine. They may also provide a far better understanding of search behavior in other engines. The exact breakdown may vary by engine, but because the data are directional, they can provide a great strategic basis for not only keyword selection but also creative development and landing page selection and design.

Since adCenter launched, MSN has been adding features that let you use the same age, gender, and geography factors to "bid boost" in order to increase your likely position for searchers for whom you're willing to pay more. Your base bid is used for any searcher for whom MSN doesn't have voluntary registration data. Don't set your base bid too low on non-targeted ads. MSN doesn't have registration data on everyone, so even some non-identified searchers may be in your sweet spot.

MSN doesn't have registration data on everyone, so even some non-identified searchers may be in your sweet spot.

Since its 2006 launch, adCenter has been adding some useful tools to its toolbox, including a handy add-in for Microsoft Excel 2007 that enables you to plan and execute your keyword strategy from within this popular productivity package. Although it's true that Microsoft's search properties aren't as popular as Google's, you shouldn't overlook this marketplace, because you should never afford to overlook an opportunity to obtain qualified search traffic.

TRUTH

15

Search engine sales versus search engine marketing

Hundreds of thousands of marketers who place Pay-Per-Click (PPC) search engine listings on Google, Yahoo!, Microsoft, and other venues think of themselves as search engine marketers. In fact, they're not behaving like search engine marketers at all. Most engage in search engine sales, not search engine marketing (SEM).

What's the difference? "Search engine sales" is a construct we'll use in this truth. In contrast to true SEM, it's a narrow-minded process in which all decisions regarding campaign optimization are made with an immediate focus on sales, regardless of other marketing goals.

Search engine sales campaigns ignore the buying cycle. They ignore the fact that some search keywords, listings, and search engines might influence sales at a later date, perhaps after another search. Because their focus is so narrow and near-term, search engine sales campaigns can result in a failure to spend enough to acquire long-term customers with high lifetime values.

For example, affiliate marketers who outsource "marketing" to affiliates (expecting the affiliates to invest their own money arbitraging PPC search results to be paid on a performance basis) don't behave like marketers at all. They outsource sales to third parties. Affiliates won't invest in advertising that results in sales through other channels or sales that are lagged, as these would be attributed to other affiliates or campaigns. The affiliates aren't behaving as marketers but as commissioned salespeople or a commission-based channel.

> ...search engine sales campaigns can result in a failure to spend enough to acquire long-term customers with high lifetime values.

The marketer benefits from the "search engine sales-think" that drives his affiliates' behavior. Marketing benefits from sales-centric advertising purchased by an affiliate based on an expected return (payout) include the following:

- Sales from dropped cookies not attributed to the affiliate

- Sales that occur after the cookie expires

58

■ Untracked offline sales

■ Overall brand lift due to ad exposure and site interaction

Even search engine "marketers" who set up campaigns based on immediate trackable sales glean the preceding unmeasured benefits. Despite these benefits, a search engine sales approach is wrong for nearly every marketer and results in far less net search profit. The reason is opportunity cost, which is the result of not doing something you could have done that would have resulted in a profit (or otherwise positive outcome).

After years of reminders from practitioners, peers, and pundits, most marketers engaged in PPC SEM have embraced metrics, measurement, and web analytics. Even more are taking proactive campaign actions based on data from campaign analytics. Increasing the breadth of these analytics to include behavior (including offline behavior) that isn't directly linked to an immediate sale or conversion provides marketers with a deeper grasp of how SEM fits in to the multichannel marketing mix.

Really visionary marketers work with internal and external technology, as well as tap experts to build more sophisticated media models to understand where search fits into integrated marketing and media plans. Insight into user behavior is required to build truly profit-maximizing plans. We know from all other media and purchase research that not all customers and prospects engage in buying behavior the same way.

Diverse targets make building integrated media models for search a bit more difficult. Yet in almost all businesses, their very best (that is, most profitable) customers have many factors in common. Zero in on these factors, learn how you acquired your very best customers, and seek out commonalities in their purchase cycles. Perhaps they evolved through the buying cycle over time and had many brand touch points prior to making a final buying decision. Additional factors to look for include the following:

■ Prepurchase research search behavior. (Most purchase decisions are preceded by two to six or more searches, according to a comScore/DoubleClick study.)

■ Competitive set. (Who else was under consideration?)

- Offline media consumption patterns and ad exposure frequency.
- PR exposure.
- Buzz exposure.

My hope is that the search engines will soon offer us the opportunity to build a media model around our best customers, determine demographics, and even boost bids for the demographic most likely to buy or, more importantly, most likely to result in a high-profit customer. In the future, it is likely that there will be opportunities to add behavioral bid increases based on how receptive to ad messages an individual has been in the past. Some inkling of what the future may hold for us is visible at Microsoft's adCenter, which offers marketers a new toolset of advanced targeting technologies (see Truth 14, "Better targeting with Microsoft adCenter").

One easy way to think about search engine sales versus search engine marketing is to regard marketing as creating interest, awareness, and demand, whereas sales fulfills only an existing demand.

If you considered yourself a search engine marketer but now realize you're operating purely in search engine sales, there's no need to panic. However, in the PPC keyword auction marketplace, if your competition uses a holistic, profit-maximizing approach to bidding while you myopically focus on immediate sales, you might think their bids are crazy. In fact, these bids may be based on a highly thought-out strategy that looks holistically at a much wider field of customer touch points and spends appropriately to reach the right people when they're in the state of mind most receptive to your message.

...if your competition uses a holistic, profit-maximizing approach to bidding while you myopically focus on immediate sales, you might think their bids are crazy.

TRUTH

16

Manage your campaigns for maximum profit

The goal of getting a positive ROI on a paid search engine marketing campaign is inherently understood. Only crazies would knowingly spend money on something with a negative return. Looking at some of the CPC prices out there these days, I think there are some crazies in our midst. Crazies aside, ROI remains a dominant buzzword in this industry.

Paradoxically, however, a campaign with the highest ROI is rarely a profit-maximizing campaign strategy. The more clients I talk to, the more I realize that the success metrics and strategies being used for search are sometimes arbitrary, and even more surprising, might not be aligned with other nonsearch marketing strategies and objectives. Admittedly, execution of search campaign optimization might be complex and daunting, but as a marketer, you have a responsibility to your company to use metrics and objectives that drive profit. In addition, whatever marketing and profit objectives you select should be consistent across media (online and offline).

Convergence just got a new meaning: Marketing, business, accounting, technology, and economics meet to optimize profit.

Warning: This can hurt your brain! MBAs have a semester of schooling to absorb the concepts that underlie the following analysis, and it has been more than 10 years since I first absorbed these concepts in an academic environment at Yale. Luckily, I liked economics, and I use these concepts every day for my own business and for clients. My objective for this truth is to explain the concepts of marginal profit and elasticity, using examples.

High ROI campaigns or ROI maximization sound wonderful, but you already know that you can't really get volume-maximizing ROI, since you have lots of listings in multiple engines. The highest ROI campaign you could have would be one where your best-converting listing is at the minimum price (CPC). The cost per order/lead/action for this listing is the lowest you can get in the search marketplace, so your ROI is maximized. For example, let's assume that for that very best listing, you spend $25 a month and drive $3,000 in sales at a 50% profit. Don't start celebrating yet. Where's the conversion volume? There isn't any. You need more traffic and should be willing to accept a lower ROI in exchange for broader, higher volume.

What you really want is a balanced approach of ROI optimization and profit maximization. Let's imagine you have the perfect balance between traffic volume and ROI, where you get high conversion volume (sales/leads/actions) and a positive profit. On a listing-by-listing basis, you are lowering per-unit profit in exchange for additional click-through/sales volume that delivers a total profit increase. If you raise your media price (CPC or CPM) too high on a particular listing, given a particular conversion rate, you get a negative profit; drop it too low, and you sacrifice more total gross profit due to the loss of additional sales/leads/actions (which is called "opportunity cost"). Economists would recommend that you continue to spend more on traffic until the incremental (marginal) profit you earn by spending more drops to zero. Of course, this is a theoretical solution, and the real world is rarely that simple.

Without extremely complex marketing automation systems, one manageable way to move to a profit-maximizing campaign management strategy is to know your cost per order/action/lead across all marketing media, as well as where that target needs to be for you to make a reasonable profit. Start by setting a specific goal CPO/CPA (cost per order or cost per action) for a campaign (or individually by listing, if listings result in different products being purchased or a different profile of the purchaser). Manage your campaign listings around that CPO/CPA goal. You'll see almost immediately which listings deliver conversion at a rate close to your CPO/CPA, simultaneously driving a high volume of conversions and traffic.

I'll assume you are doing campaign management based on some post-click conversion cost objective (automatically, or very hands on). Based on your CPO/CPA objectives, some of your listings will tend to oscillate in positions or prices close to the premium/heavily syndicated levels. For some listings, a small price increase might result in large volume changes, and this presents a profit-maximization opportunity. For example:

1. Your campaign (or group of listings) maximum CPO is set to $45.
2. Your top volume listing is delivering orders at $44.88, very close to your max.
3. That listing's position tends to be 4–6 on average, meaning that it's not heavily syndicated.
4. You get 40 orders a week at that target CPO.
5. Your net profit per sale (after subtracting the ~$45 CPO) is $40.
6. Total profit is 40 ×$40 or $1,600.

If you were to raise the target CPO for that listing to $50, then based on your conversion, you could likely raise your average position a couple of positions. Traffic would increase significantly to 90 orders a week, with a new profit per sale of $35 and a total profit of $3,150 on that listing. Your spending goes up, but you make more profit.

But wait. You don't have just one listing—you have lots of listings in many engines, plus you have other media opportunities as well. Assuming you have all the information you need to make decisions (killer analytics) and the ability to execute campaign changes smoothly and efficiently (not too much time and money spent on the processes and analysis), you can profit maximize your entire campaign at once, raising and lowering your CPO targets to find the best trade-off between volume and profit.

Finding the "right ROI" and the "profit-maximizing campaign" is where the fun begins. Convergence just got a new meaning: Marketing, business, accounting, technology, and economics meet to optimize profit. You might not have the tools and technologies that facilitate marketing automation and campaign effectiveness across media (online, direct mail, TV, print, and so on), as well as within media. In the meantime, you can use some of these concepts for your search engine marketing campaigns by implementing a combination of analytics and automation to at least maximize profit within your search campaigns.

TRUTH

17

ROI and profitability: Beyond ROAS to lifetime value and CRM

Well-executed Customer Relations Management (CRM) and customer data analytics can significantly boost revenue and profits. How do the principles of CRM apply to search engine marketing? We know that CRM and customer analytics can discover small segments of the overall customer base that contribute a disproportionate percentage of revenue or profit. You might have heard of the Pareto Principle (often called the 80-20 Rule). This principle holds true for almost every company's data. Sometimes the data is astounding, going far beyond an 80% value delivered by 20% of the customer base situation. According to research conducted in the automotive sector, the top 0.2% of all car rental customers rent 25% of all the cars.

As marketers, we must tap the power of these "super customers." To do so, we take an analytic approach that embraces the following processes:

1. Identify the "super customers" whom you already have.

2. Make sure you treat them right. (You can't afford to lose them.)

3. Determine what attributes identify those customers, setting them apart from the lower-value customers. Attributes may include psychographics, demographics, behaviors, preferences, and needs, as well as information about their tenure as customers. For the purpose of marketing optimization, the "Holy Grail" question is how these super customers became customers. Which advertising or marketing channel delivered those customers?

4. Develop a plan to grab those customers from your competition through serving the "super customer" better.

5. Capture "super customers" right at the beginning of their need for your service or product; then cultivate them and foster their loyalty.

...the "Holy Grail" question is how these super customers became customers. Which advertising or marketing channel delivered those customers?

SEM can help with competitive customer acquisition and new customer acquisition, and might even help with treating the customer right. The answer lies within analytics. I hope you are using analytics to identify the most efficient portions of your search marketing campaign, finding the keywords, engines, and listings that deliver the immediate post-click behaviors you seek (orders, registrations, or branding). Many marketers optimizing campaigns by post-click conversion behavior set their Cost Per Order (CPO) or Cost Per Action (CPA) objectives based on immediate profit on each product, shopping cart average sizes, or other short-term monetary metrics. However, you can and should go further.

Of course, consumer behaviors continue long after the initial purchase, registration, or branding experience. In the best-case scenario, that long-term behavior is what you need to track. Your mission is to determine the following:

- For e-commerce businesses, do some listings generate shopping cart averages greater than you originally estimated when setting target CPOs?

- Do some listings deliver more of those extra-value customers who continue to produce higher profit or higher revenue than average?

- Do leads from some listings deliver a greater percentage of new customers than others? This situation occurs in B2B and high-involvement purchases where the customer goes through an involved sales cycle.

- Do leads from some listings deliver new customers that order more over time? This is an attempt to look at the lifetime value of a customer.

- Do some listings deliver repeat customers (existing customers who are coming back) who don't order exclusively from you, but are reminded of you when they see a search listing? An example of this behavior is the "switcher" who is indifferent but can be persuaded by environment and price. Think Coke/Pepsi in the grocery store.

If the Pareto Principle holds true for you, a small percentage of your

If the Pareto Principle holds true for you, a small percentage of your customers deliver the lion's share of your profits.

customers deliver the lion's share of your profits. Do some of those super customers come from search listings? If a segment of your search listings deliver "super customers," doesn't this mean that these listings are more valuable? Average acquisition costs and average cost of customer acquisition can be misleading. Managing by averages might build solid business, but what if we apply the lessons learned by top CRM practitioners? What if we could determine not just our cost per order or cost per lead when managing campaigns, but also predict the lifetime value of a customer, and use that information to run a more efficient campaign?

Therein lays an opportunity to tap the power of CRM for improved efficiency. The customer has a buying cycle, and you might be communicating to them differently at each point in the buying cycle. However, for many marketers, incremental high-value customer acquisitions are possible through final stage analysis. Some eCRM and analytics companies have this capability, but a simpler analysis might provide enough information to enable you to apply CRM principles and the Pareto Principle to all your media at a much lower cost.

Set your CPO and CPA targets with the awareness that taking into account more than just immediate profit might be the optimal decision. Know the profile of your "super customer," and while you optimize for immediate profit by listing—and possibly by day-part—consider putting in place even simple analytic systems that tie back long-term behavior to all your marketing, online and off. Even if you don't have any analytics at all to support CPO/CPA decisions, sometimes your gut will lead you in the right direction. For example, let's say you sell medical supplies, and among your products are adult diapers (think Depends) and insulin test kits (the kinds of products that people have to buy repeatedly); these customers are more likely than the average customer to provide a long-term order flow. Knowing this might cause you to raise your CPO targets for some product-related listings.

Less-obvious situations include purchasers for other products, or search listings that generate unusually large shopping cart checkout totals. Do they indicate a higher lifetime value? Ask your tech team if they can do some simple user profiling: Attach the media source ID to customer IDs, and then crunch the numbers. You might get some pleasant surprises.

TRUTH

18

Missing conversions, offline conversion tracking, and SEM

On- and offline marketers often make decisions in a silo. But in a world in which customer behavior is rapidly changing, more and more CMOs and marketing VPs see the folly of separating business units that are perceived or advertised under the same brand. Clearly, consumers see the brand as one entity, even if Profit and Loss (P&L) statements and marketing budgets are maintained separately within the organization.

Study after study shows that consumers use the Internet for research when making buying decisions. comScore has conducted studies for Yahoo!, Google, and DoubleClick that track the relationship between search and buying behavior. For example, a comScore study, conducted for Google in 2006, shows that a significant 63% of those who purchased an item directly related to their search query completed the purchase offline, with just 37% making that purchase online.

This situation becomes even more fascinating when studies look at offline sales and estimate the importance of online site resources and information for purchase decisions. A Shop.org study conducted by Forrester found that 22% of offline sales are influenced by information gathered on the Web. This figure represents nearly a quarter of total offline sales, and this number will undoubtedly go up due to generational effects and the improved availability of online product information.

> If your competition isn't siloed and has determined how to measure or estimate the true impact of search on offline conversions, you'll get your you-know-what kicked....

Clearly, the percentage of your customers who rely on online information before making offline purchase decisions will vary. Each multichannel merchant must make its own decisions on how to treat the interaction effects between on- and offline shopping and preshopping behavior. The most important question for most marketers is whether the information consumers find online influences them to select one product over another, choose one brand over another, or to purchase your product from a particular retail store. If the level of influence on these kinds of decisions is high, the Web, and search in particular, become critical realms of opportunity for both retailers and manufacturers. In many cases, manufacturers might not be able to rely on the retailers to do their selling for them and might need to dramatically increase their online presence while dealing with channel conflict issues.

Of course, your data might show that even though consumers are spending time online researching products and purchases, they're not changing their behavior based on these interactions. The Web just removes friction from the product-researching process. I'm willing to bet, however, that brand, product, and store decisions are influenced by online behavior.

There are even more critical, immediate reasons why you should care if your business unit measures success based solely on measurable online conversions. Regardless of whether your online-only focus is because your business has siloed you into a separate unit or because you're currently an Internet pure play (that is, your online presence is responsible for 100% of your business), you may have a problem. If your competition isn't siloed and has determined how to measure or estimate the true impact of search on offline conversions, you'll get your you-know-what kicked, because your competition's overall conversion rate may be dramatically higher than yours, enabling them to outbid you for traffic-driving search listings. If this is the case, your only recourse is to either bid irrationally, which may get you fired (or at least in trouble), or become such a brilliant merchandiser that your landing pages convert better online than do your competitor's pages.

If you don't have serious advantages over your competitors in respect to conversion, operational cost savings, and margin, and your competitors use a holistic view of on- and offline conversion (as opposed to your myopic view of online-only conversions), you might be completely priced out of the positions with the potential to generate real scale for your business.

If you're a multichannel marketer, and either a corporate or C-level executive has empowered you to manage search based on its true value to the business (that is, net search profit), several options for gaining insight into your customers are available. One powerful product is qSearch Retail, from comScore, which extends conversion tracking among comScore panelists to offline purchase behavior. With comScore data, you can gain a powerful understanding of how search and online behavior translate into offline purchases. comScore isn't using its full online panel size for offline purchase tracking; instead, it's building smaller panels, based on specific panel member behavior, particularly for the qSearch Retail product. Panelists are then categorized by industry vertical (that is, they searched for keywords that relate to a category) and grouped ready to be surveyed should a marketer want clarity on offline purchase behavior.

You don't necessarily need comScore, however, to answer some key questions about the link between online search behavior and offline purchases. Multichannel merchants with catalogs have faced similar issue for years. Some of the catalog industry's best practices can be adapted for use in the online world, including the following:

- **Customer tagging**—Look at purchases; then marry the online cookie with the offline customer number or credit card data.

- **Offer codes**—Unique offer codes can be provided for searchers to redeem via phone or in stores.

- **Unique pricing**—Unique online pricing can also become a tracking code of its own, so when a person requests that price, she must have seen the search landing page.

- **Trackable phone numbers**—Phone sales can be routed through a tracking system similar to the VoiceXML (define) systems used for pay-per-call systems. This is great for expensive or complex purchases.

- **In-store surveys**—Survey your customers.

- **Anecdotal data**—Ask your sales associates if people show up with printouts from the website.

TRUTH

19

Search marketing as a metric

As marketers, we like to think of the entire process of search engine marketing, particularly the impressions and clicks we see from search, as a form of advertising or media. Clearly, for many aspects of our campaigns, this is true. However, the truth is far more complex than most people believe, due to the unique nature of SEM. In many cases, for many of our keywords, the search engine inventory (how many searches occur), the click-through rate on listings, and the resulting conversion rates are as much the result of non-search online and offline marketing efforts as they are products of spontaneous activity engaged in by searchers uninfluenced by external factors.

What online and offline factors have caused you to engage in searching activity? Think hard about whether your searching is spontaneous or prompted by a side effect of some part of your life. This interaction effect between advertising, marketing, PR, buzz, word of mouth, and search activity has a profound impact on the best practices in campaign management of paid search campaigns and the messaging on organic landing pages.

One way to think of this interaction effect is to view search impressions and increases in CTR as a metric of your brand recall and awareness. Changing your outlook from thinking about search purely as a cause (of orders, leads, registrations, visitors, and page views) to thinking about search as an effect can be very liberating. Whatever other marketing, advertising, PR, or CRM you do will create a change in search activity and responsiveness.

My team and I have engaged in testing and measuring the interaction effect between search and paid media with some of our larger clients (those who spend more than a million dollars a month on both search and other advertising) and have arrived at several hypotheses. These theories or hypotheses may not hold true in every case, but thus far the data has been compelling.

Before I delve into these hypotheses, imagine traditional agencies using search as an advertising success metric. If, in fact, a significant percentage of search activity is the result of external factors, clearly search impression levels and changes in click-through rate are as much a measurement or metric for the effectiveness of other media as they are the foundation of a search marketing campaign's internal metric. Because search behavior is such a high predictor of interest and eventual purchase, services such as Yahoo!'s Buzz Index (http://buzz.yahoo.com/overall/), Google Trends (http://www.google.com/trends), and custom reports from comScore, Nielsen, HitWise, and others may end up as some of the best ways to judge ad effectiveness. The hypotheses are as follows:

- **Hypothesis #1: Advertising interaction**—Some significant percentage of search activity is not spontaneous at all but is stimulated by other online or offline advertising: When a searcher searches, that search might not have been fully spontaneous but instead might be a result of exposure to advertising, direct marketing, PR, or word of mouth. All these are forms of marketing. The search activity may either be proximal to the exposure to the media, or the response to the ad message may be significantly lagged. No one formula can be expected to work for all industry segments. However, more than ever before, we can identify and track visitors based on geography, which enables us to gain an understanding not only about the effectiveness of a given SEM campaign, but also the effectiveness of local media buys and offline ad creative. If post-click conversions are the only behavior you want to link to advertising, you might not even need to change a campaign structure. However, if ad CTR is also of interest, a restructuring of your Google or Microsoft adCenter campaign makes sense. (Yahoo!'s localized campaigns are quite different and probably not worth touching for the purpose of measuring media influence.)

- **Hypothesis #2: Public relations interaction**—This hypothesis is an extension of the first and allows for the fact that some significant percentage of search activity is not spontaneous but is stimulated by public relations, buzz, or news. When building a media measurement model that attempts to measure the first hypothesis, it might be prudent to also measure PR nationally or within geographical segments.

- **Hypothesis #3: Word-of-mouth buzz**—They used to call it viral marketing. Now they call it word of mouth (WOM) or buzz marketing. No matter what you call it, the buzz generated when prospects and customers talk about your company or product can be a powerful influence on search behavior and, therefore, on your search campaign. Word-of-mouth buzz could initially be

75

stimulated or generated by PR or advertising, or might be caused by the product itself. Think about Google's first four years, a period in which it grew almost exclusively based on WOM. So if you are going to use search as a metric of success for other forms of marketing, don't neglect the potential impact of WOM buzz.

- **Hypothesis #4: Search behavior is stimulated by searching—** Our own data and data reported by comScore show that consumers engage in long strings of searches as they move down the purchase decision funnel. Our hypothesis is that both search impressions and engagement with a marketer's site act to stimulate additional search behavior. When the advertiser's site has been engaged with, this hypothesis postulates that future search interaction is positively weighted toward the brand/site that had the initial engagement. This behavior corresponds with classic buy funnel behavior.

Not many marketers are ready to use search as a metric of success for all their various media and PR campaigns. However, knowing about the interaction effects between media enables a good SEM agency or in-house search team to leverage all the other media and marketing campaigns to improve SEM campaign efficiency and effectiveness.

TRUTH

Branding metrics for SEM

Search marketing is generally considered a direct marketing medium. However, consumers use search throughout their decision-making process, making it critical that marketers take a more holistic view of their behavior. Through the use of metrics that correlate with eventual purchases, marketers can apply the rigorous trackability of consumers' post-click behavior to make sure budgets are spent effectively, not just to harvest existing demand, but also to influence future buying decisions.

Brand marketers already have an advantage in their ability to maximize the volume of clicks received from both the algorithmic and PPC search engines. But it's not all roses. When it comes to using metrics to measure effectiveness and adjust a search campaign accordingly, the branders have it tough. Sure, search engine text listings have some branding impact. However, it is more likely that brand advertisers are interested in creating a branding experience on their sites, which is reckoned using a post-click metric.

Search engine marketers must use easily measurable data that correlate well with branding metrics to make the necessary, ongoing adjustments to their SEM campaigns. To advance this process, I'd like to suggest a new metric based on a behavior mapping strategy. I call it the Branding Effectiveness Index, or BEI, pronounced "buy." Although the BEI concept is a work in progress, it has already been quite useful in comparing SEM campaign results for many of our clients.

> Websites impact the brand, and marketers should plan and adjust their campaigns based on brand-awareness measurements.

Traditional branding metrics that marketing research firm Dynamic Logic uses for an online environment are Aided Brand Awareness, Brand Favorability/Behavior Intent, and Message Association. These metrics are designed for measuring the branding impact of an ad. In our case, the site itself is doing the branding, so we must turn to the following proxies to build our own BEI:

- Purchase (yes, we can use purchase; see the McDonald's example later)

- Registration
- Newsletter subscription
- Information request
- Pageview
- Content depth or involvement
- Webinar view

To generate your own BEI, set the most valuable measurable action to a value of 1. Then assign a percentage value to all other significant actions based on their relative importance. For example, if a brochure request is considered 70% as important as a newsletter registration, assign the former a value of 0.7. All the actions are added up and multiplied by their importance factor. These are then totaled and divided by spending to get the BEI. Once established, any campaign or segment of a campaign (even a single keyword listing) can then be measured based on how well it did on achieving a BEI. Using the preceding example, 20 newsletter registrations and 10 newsletter requests achieved by spending \$1,000 result in a BEI of 0.027 $((20^*1)+(10^*.7))/1000$. If the number of newsletter registrations goes up to 40 for a different campaign segment, the BEI becomes 0.047. This value is very useful for comparing segments of a campaign when using the same formula. However, if you have a second campaign with a different set of measurable actions, the results will not be comparable. A simpler way to think of my BEI is as a variable such as a weighted average CPA (cost per action), incorporating a host of post-click actions.

Let's look at some of the Ad Age's Top Megabrands to see what metrics they might use to build a BEI, as follows:

- **AT&T**—The corporate site has the business units identified and also provides some general tools for visitors. It is unlikely that AT&T would send paid SE traffic to the corporate page, so let's look at their consumer site. If customer acquisition is the highest valued action, that value is set to 1, the loyalty program signup might be set at 0.4, and interaction with a plans and services page might be set at 0.15.
- **Verizon**—Verizon has some similarities to AT&T but has a host of other actions it could use to build a BEI. There is no limit to how many actions combine to create the BEI; it is limited only by the marketer's ability to measure.

- **Chevrolet**—Chevrolet has a brochure request, a dealer locator, and a Contact Us form, as well as content and a strange clubs listing that is difficult to find. One could combine these measurable actions together to form an overall BEI. If the most desirable action is use of the dealer locator, that is assigned a value of 1, with each of the other potential actions assigned a differing value as a percentage. For example, if a brochure request is considered 70% as important as use of the dealer locator, assign that a value of 0.7.
- **Ford**—Ford seems to place an emphasis on newsworthy information, such as a special financing rate. Perhaps that would be its most important metric in building its BEI, or perhaps a visit to the "Build Your Ford" area.
- **Toyota**—Toyota is currently pushing several fuel-efficient vehicles on its site and might use interaction with those brands' pages as a large factor in the BEI. If there is an event such as a pageview that is likely to repeat, it can be assigned a BEI factor relative to another less frequent action. Different pages can be assigned different factors as well. The sweepstakes entry might have a factor of 1, and the pageviews within a particular model's section a factor of 0.03 for each pageview.
- **McDonald's**—McDonald's has a restaurant locator and might assign that the factor of 1, assign purchase of merchandise at 0.9, and assign visits to the "Treasure Planet Happy Meal" area of the site a factor of 0.2.

Whether you think my BEI is a wonderful new way of combining existing metrics together to capture the branding impact of a site, or the nonsensical ravings of a guy who has looked at too much data, the fact remains that websites impact the brand, and marketers should plan and adjust their campaigns based on brand awareness measurements. My branding clients are happy to have an empirical way to effectively manage their paid search campaigns.

TRUTH

21

Search and the buying cycle

Are you always ready to buy, ready to register, ready to call, and ready to subscribe? I didn't think so. Neither is your target audience. Remember Marketing 101 or those sales books that talk about the buying cycle? They have a point well worth heeding when it comes to search marketing: Not every visitor is ready to buy all the time, and that doesn't mean they are worthless to you; quite the contrary, they might be close to becoming a valuable customer.

Normally, I rant and rave about measuring conversion so that you can optimize your campaign around orders, monetizable actions, and conversions to leads. However, CPOs, CPAs, and "lifetime value" are just the beginning of the story for many marketers. Marketers must embrace the reality that the stages of the buying cycle must be taken into account when planning and executing search marketing campaigns. Prospects within your target audience go though phases in the buying cycle online, just as they would offline. To ignore this fact results in an inefficient site and an inefficient media campaign, regardless of traffic source (that is, search traffic, banners, or other media). Depending on your role within your organization, you might think of these "not ready to buy" phases differently. A common definition of the buying cycle used by sales enthusiasts is attention, interest, conviction, desire, and close. Some marketers prefer to use a definition of the "marketing cycle" or "marketing life cycle," and will use the acronym AIDA for Attention, Interest, Desire, and Action. CRM marketers have their own steps— reach, acquisition, conversion, retention, loyalty—while branders use lift in metrics like "unaided awareness" and "purchase intent." At the end of the day, all these metrics are attempting to quantify, measure, or at least acknowledge that the customer goes through stages, and that to be efficient marketers, we need to keep the buying process in mind when planning and executing campaigns. The same is true for search campaigns—and perhaps even more so, because those CPCs are getting high, and you need to know if they are worth it.

> Not every visitor is ready to buy all the time, and that doesn't mean they are worthless to you....

As a manufacturer or brander, you definitely want to reach consumers in the early stages of their buying cycle. As a retailer, your preference might be to catch consumers after they have passed through the early stages of the cycle and are ready to buy, or are at least ready to register for a specials newsletter. So the level to which you take into account the early stages of the buying cycle depends on your overall marketing objectives. There are two ways to factor in the early stages of the cycle—one is more quantitative, and the other more qualitative.

The quantitative method of factoring the buying cycle in a SEM campaign would be to use survey data or other information about user behaviors post-click to telegraph what stages of the buying cycle that the visitor is in. For example, you could use a blended post-click behavior metric such as BEI (see Truth 20, "Branding metrics for SEM"), where you assign different post-click behavior values based on their impact on the visitor's likelihood to buy (and therefore their value to you). By using this blended metric as your optimization objective, and adjusting the values of the different activities, you can adjust price or position of each listing in your campaign based on the traffic's true value to you. Each listing delivers a mix of immediate buyers and those in earlier stages of the buying cycle, as well as a few completely disinterested people who clicked on a listing without reading it carefully. By taking buying stages into account, you optimize for the true value of a campaign. The challenge is in setting the values of actions so that they accurately reflect the value to your organization. Brand marketers might do an intercept survey to determine what actions on their site resulted in a lift in "purchase intent" or "awareness." A direct marketer might use hard data, attributing a value to a catalog request or a newsletter registration based on how many of those requestors actually purchase on average.

The qualitative way to address the early stage versus late stage visitor is to use linguistic logic. For example, let's illustrate a typical search marketing campaign containing a variety of keywords; some will likely indicate the mindset of the searcher sufficiently to adjust your CPC for that keyword to reflect early stage visitors who you still value at some level:

- "Laser printer" (generic term—might be a mix of early stages and might be ready to buy).
- "Laser printer review" or "laser printer compare" (likely not quite ready to buy; however, might be susceptible to marketing messages that concern benefits of a particular unit).
- "Cheap laser printer" (probably close to the purchase stage but price sensitive).
- "Best laser printer" (likely not quite ready to buy; however, might be susceptible to marketing messages that concern benefits of a particular unit).
- "Hp 1200 laser printer" (might be close to purchase due to the use of a specific model number).

Should you start valuing your site visitors differently? That depends on your business and if you are likely to be the beneficiary of the attitude or preference changes you facilitated during the early buying stages. You don't want to contribute to someone's buying cycle if they buy from your competition, but you might want to do so if you are a multichannel retailer and you have data that indicates that research done online results in an offline purchase though YOUR retail outlet. Of course, manufacturers benefit themselves as well as their distribution channels when they use search engine marketing, regardless of whether you call it branding, building awareness, lifting purchase intent, competitive positioning, or facilitating the sales cycle.

TRUTH

22

Branding opportunities in keywords

Some brand marketers are already involved with search, but those new to the medium should enter and buy listings to enhance their on- and offline branding campaigns. For some of the largest brands, inventory levels for most search words directly attributed to their brands are quite low. Even Coke and Pepsi see only monthly searches in the 100,000 range for their brands, and nearly none for generic terms such as "cola" and "thirst quencher." Even if Click-Through Rates (CTRs) reach 10%, search spending and the total impressions represent only a comparative drop in brand marketers' buckets.

One way to expand a campaign is to associate brands with the problems they solve or attributes they want to portray ("grass stain," "sexy car," "healthy meal," "clear cellular," "fast meal," and so on). The upside of this strategy is that the brand marketer increases unaided awareness at the precise time searchers are open to a message regarding a solution to their problem. The downside is that there really isn't much inventory available for purchase, because there are only so many keywords describing the kind of problem likely to be solved by such products.

However, brand marketers eager to capitalize on a search listing's capability to increase brand awareness do have an alternative to limiting their selection to low-volume keywords. For instance, many major brands sponsor sports or entertainment events. Query volume on sports and entertainment keywords typically runs high. In some cases, the CPC for keywords associated with sports, sports personalities, TV shows, movie characters, or actors are reasonable compared to average CPC. If the brand has relevant content on its site (or can generate it inexpensively), the promotion sponsorship keywords (PSKs) are

> One way to expand a campaign is to associate brands with the problems they solve or attributes they want to portray.

a powerful branding opportunity, particularly when coupled with the Branding Effectiveness Index (BEI) I have devised (see Truth 20, "Branding metrics for SEM"). Brand marketers should look at PSKs the same way as promotions: The PSKs extend the promotion's or sponsorship's value and multiply the brand's visibility in relation to the original promotion, sports event, person, or entertainment.

Here are some examples of how marketers can use PSKs:

Coke could buy *American Idol*, the judges' names, and all the stars' names, as well as the NASCAR personalities' names. Coke spends a reported $25 million per season to associate itself with *American Idol*. It's natural for searchers to associate Coke with the show, and a site with relevant content would provide an unparalleled branding experience for those conducting searches on the show and its stars.

Here are some additional examples that I think would be effective:

- If Coke didn't buy the clicks, perhaps Ford or Cingular (becoming once again AT&T) should take up the slack.
- Hewlett-Packard could buy *Shrek* terms, as well as Magic Johnson. (HP works with his foundation.)
- Buick or Accenture could buy Tiger Woods and other related golf terms.
- Callaway, PING, and Nike should all buy the names of the pro golfers who use their equipment, as well as the names of their caddies.
- McDonald's should buy "Neopets," "Tony Hawk," "LPGA," Olympic keywords, and World Cup terms.
- Nike should buy "Serena Williams," "Michael Jordan," and all Olympic-related terms, including major athletes' names.

When buying personalities as keywords, it's important to monitor the news, just in case external events could create negative brand associations (for example, Martha Stewart for Kmart, Kobe Bryant for McDonald's, or Whoopi Goldberg for Slim-Fast). Although the opportunity exists for brand marketers to leverage the power of SEM through a variety of means, the campaigns must be monitored actively and vigilantly.

Brand marketers aren't the only ones bidding on their own brand keywords. Both the channel and the competition might also bid on brand names in Google. Some product brands are heavily bid upon by retailers authorized to sell that brand's products. Pampers, iPod, ThinkPad, QuickBooks, and CoolPix are all sold by retailers with online presences. Corvette, F-150, and Chris-Craft are bid on by sales channels for those brands. Brand owners must decide if they want to bid on these keywords, regardless of whether they themselves have an online store.

The decision by the brand holder to bid when there is already an active channel and that brand does not sell direct is not a trivial one. Most retailers and other channel partners (in travel, insurance, and web hosting) are not exclusive to one brand. Therefore, there is a real risk that the retailer will capture a customer on one brand term and inadvertently sell a competing brand. In that case, the brand has ceded control to third parties and runs the risk of losing a customer permanently if a cross-sell to another brand occurs.

Some brand marketers might believe they can coast along on high organic rankings, but this course can be risky, especially in cases where effective organic position rates are depressed by other elements competing for scarce SERP real estate. Furthermore, relying on organic listings alone deprives the marketer of a powerful opportunity to establish a marketing touch point (perhaps with complementary messaging) that is tailored for searchers who have already demonstrated an understanding of a given brand's equity. Conversely, as competing marketers learn how to tap the power of their competitors' brands when those brands generate searches that might not be favorable to your client's trademarks, it will become increasingly important for the brand holders to consider the possible negative impact of remaining passive in the paid search marketplace. I anticipate some changes in marketing budgets as brands realize they are giving huge gifts to their competition by staying out of paid search.

Some brand marketers might believe they can coast along on high organic rankings....

TRUTH

23

Paying for shelf space in the search supermarket

Sometimes, it's useful to consider PPC SEM from a new perspective, particularly when it comes to explaining to others what exactly paid placement means to marketers. Marketers struggle with understanding both the short- and long-term effect search placements have on purchase and sales. One analogy I've been mulling over recently is that of slotting fees and retailers' practice of charging for shelf space. As I thought more about grocery stores and how products are marketed in them, I found significant parallels between in-store advertising, promotional marketing, slotting allowances as a whole, and overall SEM, both organic and paid.

These parallels may help you explain SEM to a senior executive who perhaps doesn't live and breathe SERPs and real-time keyword auctions the way search marketers do. Although there are no perfect analogies for SEM, we need a handy arsenal of appropriate analogies when discussing SEM with senior managers who haven't delved into the nuts and bolts of search. The slotting or shelf space analogy might be perfect. Let's look at all the ways it works:

- Visibility correlates with action. Stores know final purchase decisions are often made at the point of purchase. Visibility influences purchases, particularly among shoppers with no strong brand preference. This allows retailers (particularly grocers) to charge manufacturers slotting allowances. Essentially, this translates into an increased guaranteed margin for the retailer.

- Shoppers arrive with the intent to purchase, particularly in grocery stores (perhaps not in stores where shopping can be considered entertainment). In

Some brands are so strong that consumers expect them to have high visibility.

SEM, consumers arrive with a question. Search engines make money from an existing demand for information. Sure, searchers can become more curious and search more aggressively to find exactly what they're looking for, but searchers rarely spontaneously search; instead, they're driven by some external force or influence (marketing, advertising, PR, buzz, news, educational interest, or, in rare cases, spontaneous curiosity).

- Some brands are so strong that consumers expect them to have high visibility. Stores must comply with this expectation. Some advertisers have built brands that are so strong that the retailer must give the brand good placement or risk losing customers. Similarly, search engines tune ranking algorithms to make sure that unless something's horribly wrong, the top results for general category searches are known brands. Consumers expect to see them. In searches for the brand itself, consumer expectation is 100%.

- There's both an immediate and a lagged outcome of increased visibility. When stores use end caps to promote a particular product (often one that's on sale and heavily promoted), consumers become more aware of it. There's a residual effect on sales (both repeat sales and sales likely influenced by high promotion visibility). In PPC search, not every searcher is ready to buy. Several public studies have quantified lagged on- and offline conversions in which search clearly played a role in final product selection or retailer selection (on- or offline). Marketers have learned to quantify the delayed effect of in-store promotions and slotting allowance spending. The same efforts must be made to understand search's role in buying decisions over a long period, including the interaction effects with other media.

- If you don't pay the slotting allowance or advertise in-store, your competition will. In SEM, there's always someone ready to take your position if you can't afford it or drop out.

> If you don't pay the slotting allowance or advertise in-store, your competition will.

- Many marketers feel pressure to pay slotting allowances or spend on in-store media simply because their competition does. Paid search competition for position is often driven by an irrational need to match or fight the competition for position with no regard to how to best allocate limited budgets.

- Consumers usually aren't aware of slotting allowances. Similarly, many searchers don't know sponsored listings are paid for by advertisers. In a recent survey performed by Didit Labs, more than 43% of respondents answered "no" when asked whether they had ever clicked on a sponsored link, even though they had to click on a sponsored link to respond to the survey. An even smaller percentage of searchers understand the lengths to which marketers go to manipulate organic listings using organic SEO optimization tactics. Of course, there's nothing pristine or pure about organic listings; they're simply manifestations of an algorithm. Most factors that contribute to relevancy scores in the organic environment are well understood by marketers, but again, most consumers have a very poorly developed understanding about the way SERP listings are achieved.

■ Consumers are aware of in-store advertising, particularly promotional advertising. Similarly, ad copy in paid-placement search results has become quite promotional, signaling to consumers that they're being advertised to.

When the CEO or marketing VP asks you why SEM budgets need to grow, perhaps the previous analogy will help explain why it pays to be in the SERPs, both for immediate ROI and because search so strongly affects consumers as they make their buying decisions.

TRUTH

24

Brand discounts at the major search engines

The hybrid auction systems used by all the major search engines reward brands and compelling, relevant creative. This brand discount lets marketers achieve higher positions on SERPS at lower bids.

Why the discount? Searchers like to click on ads that are familiar, relevant, and compelling. Although this discount has existed for years within Google's AdWords system, in the past several years, it has become more pronounced, especially due to the fact that Google's Quality Score system plays such an important role in determining SERP positions and keyword prices. Put simply, Quality Score takes into account factors beyond historical CTR when calculating the predicted CTR for a particular ad in a specific situation (for example, match type, geography, length of search query, and so on). A brand term is a powerful factor, which influences predicted CTR, regardless of position. Brand terms should be used in the ad copy or in a branded domain for the landing page URL section of the listing.

...better, more relevant ad creative will result in a higher CTR, which may put you on par with the branded competition.

When purchasing media or writing marketing plans, brand advertisers often think of target customers from a demographics perspective. Microsoft's adCenter was the first search engine to take this into account by allowing marketers to "bid boost" by age and gender. Brand marketers love this feature, and, over time, direct marketers will, too, if they can determine whether certain age and gender combinations result in higher conversions.

Major brands, as well as sellers of their products and services, can take advantage of this brand discount. But marketers who lack a strong brand need not despair. If you don't sell brands and aren't a brand in your own right (that is, having a domain people will recognize and associate with your product or service), you can always hope your competition makes some tactical or strategic errors or writes ads that are so boring and generic that even with the brand effect, your ads are more exciting and compelling. Better yet, you can use the following tactics to level the playing field, effectively compensating for the brand discount you don't receive. Tactics include the following:

- Developing better ad creative (tuned to the specific keywords searchers use). Having better, more relevant ad creative will result in a higher CTR, which might put you on par with the branded competition.
- Having a domain name that includes the keyword or category mentioned in the search ad listing. You'll get more clicks because eye-scanning behavior demonstrates that searchers quickly absorb the keyword or related concepts in the domain and act upon it.
- Using the relevant keyword in the ad creative.
- Buying more "longer tail" keywords (keywords that are seldom searched upon). The keyword "tail" contains less frequently searched keywords that you might want to mine for value. If you do this successfully, you might capture search traffic your branded competitor may be missing.
- Raising your bid and spending the money to brand experientially. Although your competition likely has spent millions (or perhaps billions) of dollars to build its brand in off- and online media, many memorable brands (for example, TMZ.com, *The Huffington Post*, and of course Google itself) have been built from scratch in cyberspace. Perhaps spending a few thousand more in PPC search will build such a brand by attracting people to your site and making it a "must visit each day" waystation on the Web.
- Improving your conversion rate. If you can get your conversion rate up a couple percentage points, you will be able to afford a higher bid. This higher bid might be required to compensate for your branded competitor's high CTR.

Brands have clear advantages in PPC search.

Brands have clear advantages in PPC search. If you're a brand marketer, it's a reason to rejoice. If you aren't, you must be smarter and more nimble to outmaneuver the brands you compete with. Of course, if you have a few million dollars to spare, you might consider building a brand of your own using a combination of SEM and traditional media buys.

TRUTH

25

Dirty data equals bad bids

Garbage in; garbage out. This saying, from the early days of data processing, illustrates the fact that even the most brilliant computer program can't deliver when poor data are fed into the system. Well, the problem hasn't gone away; in fact, it is far more serious today because many search marketing campaigns are based on garbage data.

A huge segment of marketers base their entire bid strategy on bad data. Sometimes, reasonably good data is incorrectly interpreted in respect to bid intelligence. Marketers and agencies seem to focus heavily on the bidding process when it comes to managing paid placement search campaigns. Often, data used to make these bidding decisions is assumed to be the right kind when, in fact, it's only surface data. None of it accurately reflects actual business and marketing objectives.

Situations in which the wrong or inadequate data are collected include the following:

> **A huge segment of marketers base their entire bid strategy on bad data.**

- **Solely collecting binary data when numerical data would be far more valuable**—This happens when an order or lead had been generated with no additional information about that order or lead being collected. Sure, you might be managing around a Cost-Per-Action/acquisition (CPA) or Cost-Per-Order (CPO), but chances are your business is driven by factors other than mere averages.

- **Focusing only on a single conversion event without recognizing that the prospect, consumer, or buyer goes through a more complex buying cycle**—Not every visitor is ready to buy. In reality there are many micro-conversions that lead to the final purchase. The idea is to influence eventual purchase (see Truth 21, "Search and the buying cycle").

- **Missing opportunities for data richness or data pass-back**—Better campaign management and web analytics systems/ solutions can benefit from additional data relating to marketing objectives. For example, passing back zip code, customer score, new/returning customer, or gender data can be important, particularly now that several search engines allow for bid boost/targeting by demographics. Additionally, Google's Site Targeting network tool allows site selection based on visitors' demographic profiles.

■ **Failure to test search-specific buy funnel behavior**—If your site is like most others, most search visitors (even those arriving on product or brand keywords) don't immediately buy during their first session. For example, let's say that someone typed in a search term that flagged him as interested in what you have to offer, but didn't visibly consummate a sale or otherwise engage in one of your preferred positive (success) behaviors. If your site had a positive impact on this visitor, he might return some time in the future via the following:

  • An organic search listing generated by either a new keyword or the same keyword

  • A paid search listing generated by either a new keyword or the same keyword

  • Direct navigation or bookmark

  • Other media

■ **Neglecting the organic placement/paid placement interaction effects**—Savvy marketers know how to maximize profit when they have top organic rankings. Usually, this involves using paid search to provide alternative messaging to searchers while increasing their presence in the available screen real estate. Any cannibalization or interaction effects between the paid and organic listings can be tested due to the control you have over the paid listings.

■ **Neglecting to include offline conversion**—Study after study shows that most retail conversions to a sale occur offline, after search engines were used to make a product or vendor selection.

Another problem that marketers face is when the data collection methodology is somehow flawed, or the way data are managed creates issues that must be taken into account when running search campaigns. Flaws in data collection methodology arise from a combination of human error, site-side technology issues, and third-party analytics or campaign management technology bugs. Common issues resulting in flawed, inaccurate data include the following:

- **Missing tracking codes/bugs/pixels**—Make sure you have a quality control process that verifies pixels are deployed on all the right pages and ensures that the right information is passed into third-party technology applications.

- **Setting your campaign management objectives without taking into account the ongoing problem of cookie deletion due to spyware and manual paranoia**—There is no such thing as perfect tracking of online or offline media. So keep in mind the difference between measured conversion and ROI and the likely true ROI that is nearly impossible to measure.

- **Failing to tag keywords individually within the engines**—This can result in a loss of understanding of the campaign's linguistic drivers.

- **Failing to analyze referrers on inbound search traffic**—This can result in an inability to separate the phrases that arise from a broad match listing.

- **Not tagging contextual search traffic as separately identifiable**—Failing to do this can result in an inability to know the relative ROI of search and contextual parts of a search engine's network.

- **Not capturing time/date information in a click**—Without time and date information, day-parting cannot be successfully implemented.

Any data relevancy or data quality issues can completely derail a campaign, regardless of how much energy is put into bid management. Bid and campaign management systems rely on the data they collect (or are fed).

Garbage in. Garbage out. Take the time to ensure that your campaign is empowered by accurate, relevant data and not crippled by wrong or inaccurate information.

TRUTH

26

Should you be using
web analytics to manage
search?

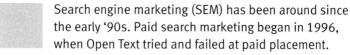

Search engine marketing (SEM) has been around since the early '90s. Paid search marketing began in 1996, when Open Text tried and failed at paid placement. GoTo (which became Overture and is now incorporated into Yahoo! Search Marketing) succeeded a year later. Paid placement sparked a search marketing revolution. Hundreds of thousands of marketers added search to integrated marketing plans. But despite the widespread adoption of paid search, there's still confusion among marketers regarding how best to execute a search marketing campaign, particularly one that meets specific goals or objectives.

Much of the confusion is over campaign tracking and optimization. All campaign optimization starts with tracking, of course. Tracking documents which engine, keyword/listing, price, position, and creative combinations deliver specific results—but that's just the beginning of a successful campaign. Tracking, although necessary, doesn't create a successful, efficient campaign.

Marketing teams (or software) crunch tracking data using analytics. Then, the teams take considered, accurate, and appropriate actions at the right time. The right action at the right time is the essence of optimization. Optimization decisions are based on specific objectives and goals, knowing where you are now and where you want to be.

Several types of analytic functionality enable you to combine conversion statistics with cost data to calculate return on investment (ROI). From this, an action plan can be charted. Following is an overview of leading companies offering analytic functionality, categorized by type. It is by no means comprehensive but will assist you in evaluating options.

Third-party ad serving

Ad-serving companies, used by clients and agencies for years, can keep track of media-buy clicks and post-click behavior. These products and services are designed for online marketing tracking and management. CPC or CPM data is entered into these tools to provide ROI metrics. All the players currently offer solutions across media types. They have rich media and text link tracking support. The major players are the following:

- **Atlas DMT**—The Atlas website says, "Our end-to-end solution enables you to plan, serve, analyze, and manage successful online campaigns." Atlas (now owned by Microsoft) offers a suite of solutions providing targeting, scheduling, and analytics.
- **Bluestreak**—Bluestreak (recently bought by Aegis) describes itself as a "global online direct marketing firm." Its Ion service provides "full-service third-party ad serving that simplifies the processes and improves the results of online marketing."
- **DoubleClick's DART**—The DoubleClick site lists a primary feature as "track results beyond impressions and clicks to understand conversion, ROI, and branding." DoubleClick's DART (along with DoubleClick's other assets) was acquired by Google.
- **Mediaplex's Adserver**—Mediaplex describes the product as "the most advanced technology available for managing online advertising workflow and increasing campaign effectiveness." Mediaplex has a range of products that perform analytics, automated scheduling, and conversion reporting.

Web analytics vendors

Web analytics firms evolved from a background of general visitor tracking and have added media tracking during their evolution. Many do not have graphical media serving technology to facilitate serving banners or rich media, but they all have visitor tracking. Each tool has its own features, functionality, and strengths. Costs vary. You should use a web analytics firm even if you also use a third-party ad server. The top analytics firms (alphabetically) are as follows:

- **Coremetrics**—Coremetrics analytics are user profile-centric. Its description reads, "Coremetrics Marketforce for Retail is the only web analytics platform that captures and stores all visitor and customer clickstream activity." Its Marketing Management Center offers reports designed around marketing tracking and reporting.
- **Fireclick**—Fireclick Netflame takes pride in its unique, graphical reporting interface. It describes itself as a "cost-effective, simple

103

solution for increasing traffic, conversion rates, and profitability by addressing all aspects of customer experience on the Web, from navigation and design to campaign tracking and promotion effectiveness."

■ **NetIQ's WebTrends**—The diehard of the web analytics business, WebTrends has expanded by creating an analysis tool that works on existing log files to include a remote ASP solution. Its site describes the newer product as "allowing you to optimize your media mix including SEM, improve web site conversion, and segment your most valuable visitors for repeat business."

■ **Omniture**—Omniture places significant emphasis on testing and optimizing nonmedia elements, as well as allowing inbound traffic to be tagged and identified. Its newest platform, SiteCatalyst 9.0, is described as "unprecedented features previously unavailable in the analytics industry that immediately enable enterprise companies to gain insight into unique online customer segments, make educated decisions, and thereby improve business processes and ROI."

■ **Unica**—Unica offers two products (Affinium NetInsight and NetTracker) tailored for enterprise-level and small web businesses, which provide advanced analytical capabilities.

■ **WebSideStory**—WebSideStory's HitBox may be best known for low-end page counters and basic reports, but it also offers high-end solutions. "HitBox helps you track, analyze, and optimize the performance of your online initiatives."

Several larger affiliate marketing solutions include tracking and might offer a module that meets your needs.

Evaluating needs

When evaluating vendors, remember that in order to evaluate search campaigns, one must combine tracking data (showing conversion percentages and behaviors) with cost data. That's how you arrive at success metrics. Often these are ROI-type metrics such as Cost Per Order (CPO), Cost Per Action (CPA), or Return on Advertising Spending (ROAS). After determining the ROI or efficiency of each listing, you need to make decisions and optimize based on these metrics.

TRUTH

27

Who's watching the bids?

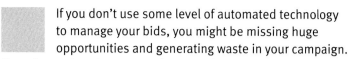

If you don't use some level of automated technology to manage your bids, you might be missing huge opportunities and generating waste in your campaign. Even the engines have started to provide controls that can be used as some form of bid management. Automated bid management isn't a panacea. Used wrongly, such systems can easily drive your campaign into budget-wasting territory. Bid management technology is only as good as its programmer/designer and the human operator at its controls.

> Used wrongly, automated bid management systems can easily drive your campaign into budget-wasting territory.

Why automation matters

I'm amazed by how many marketers continue to manage search with a spreadsheet and pivot table. And those spreadsheet jockeys seem advanced in comparison to marketers using far less-sophisticated tactics. My business partner just had a $1-million-per-month spender tell him that his "special strategy" is to be number one on every keyword. I'm sure Google, Yahoo!, and Microsoft are very pleased they have advertisers for whom position is the objective, not the means to deliver scale at acceptable profit levels!

Although it's true that the human beings running your search campaign—their brains and expertise—are critical factors in the continued success and growth of your campaign, even the best brains need help doing the "heavy lifting" of managing bids within the engines' real-time auction systems.

Search engine-provided bid management systems

Search marketers have long complained to the search engines that web-based bidding interfaces are difficult to work with and third-party bid management solutions come up short. The complaints have been particularly loud from smaller and less-sophisticated search marketers. Search engines, in response, have increased automation even while becoming more complex due to additional targeting options. Two of the big three search engines have rolled out rudimentary bid management systems, as follows:

- **Google's Conversion Optimizer**—Google's Conversion Optimizer is essentially a bid management product. You set a CPA and use the Google conversion tracking pixel. The system will then attempt to manage to your CPA goal. Google describes the Conversion Optimizer as "an AdWords feature that manages your advertising costs around specific conversion goals." Google has supposedly added some fairly advanced logic into its system that only some high-end bid and campaign management technologies possess. For example, many off-the-shelf bid management systems don't factor in conversion differences by match type, geographic location, and Google network partner.
- **Yahoo!'s Campaign Optimizer**—Yahoo!'s Campaign Optimization was rolled out concurrently with the launch of its Panama system in February of 2007, but wasn't initially turned on by default. Similar to Google's more recent launch of Conversion Optimizer, Yahoo!'s system optimizes around success metrics that you set. The engine boasts of efficiency gains that are probably excessively optimistic. According to the site, "Campaign Optimization can help you spend your campaign's budget as efficiently as possible based on your business objectives (that is, if you want to achieve a certain cost-per-click or return-on-ad-spend figure) or guidelines (for example, the value and importance of impressions, clicks, and conversions/revenue)."

Google's and Yahoo!'s automated bid-management systems are one-size-fits-all solutions. But great campaign management goes far beyond managing bids. My team and I have found that even businesses in the same industry category often have significantly different success metrics and key performance indicators, so any standard tool will generally not be customizable enough.

When to use a third-party system

There are many SEM agencies offering bid management tools and full-service packages that include the services of a skilled team trained in the tool's proper operation. As someone who was intimately involved in developing one of the first bid management systems and witnessed the bid landscapes evolve, I've tested

107

and incorporated dozens of different approaches into a bidding algorithm. Here are some questions to ask:

- How rapidly do you want it to react if conditions may be trending positively?
- If certain patterns repeat, can the system learn?
- Does the system work as well in volatile keyword markets as it does in stagnant ones?
- Can the system detect or test the elasticity of your marketplace to determine if upside opportunities exist at a very low incremental marginal predicted cost (slightly higher CPA)?

Regardless of whether a marketer prefers a simple or complex portfolio model or a more nuanced data-driven segmentation model, the bidding engine should have two characteristics. It should have the capability to be set up to be predictive. (Some call this a learning algorithm.) The algorithm must also be reactive. Reactivity is akin to the program trading software on Wall Street that reacts to a change in the financial ecosystem.

Reactivity can be important in many ways. For example, a marketer bidding on the keyword "Janet Jackson" several years ago would have seen her conversion rate (and potentially her Quality Score) drop precipitously as the makeup of search intent changed during the infamous wardrobe malfunction episode. The same can happen to any company, based on the flow of news items or changes in search behavior.

Marketers with simple businesses might find there's a fit between their bid management needs and Google's and Yahoo!'s solutions. Others will opt for third-party solutions. When you evaluate bid management, remember it focuses exclusively on buying clicks. Winning at search requires not only that you buy the most profitable clicks, but that you also continuously refine campaigns for maximum conversion and profitability.

TRUTH

28

The click fraud conundrum

To determine if a click is fraudulent or invalid, one needs to define a click. Easy, right? Perhaps not. The reports on the magnitude of click fraud vary dramatically. Similarly, the data on overall click quality and which factors tend to correlate highly with quality are scarce. (Many organizations, including my own, have done their own analyses.) Everyone's jumping on this bandwagon. So, I'll focus on the most basic premise: the click. What is a click, and when should a marketer be charged for one? Similarly, when should publishers be paid for one?

The crux of the click fraud issue is marketers shouldn't have to pay for clicks that aren't authentic or valid. A tangential issue is what other clicks might not be suitable as media and, therefore, shouldn't be paid for. The goal seems to be to define and determine what a billable click is. Even if we can achieve a black-and-white definition of a click or a billable click, we're left with the challenge of measuring and validating those clicks.

Toward that end, several major Internet advertising players are attacking these issues. The Search Engine Marketing Professional Organization (SEMPO) is supporting a Fair Isaac Corp. study of click quality. It will attempt to understand the click fraud and click quality problem. Researchers are calling for participants, so if you want a personalized, confidential report (whether you're the advertiser, a web analytics provider, or an agency), contact these firms and consider participating. You'll also gain access to the public report.

The Interactive Advertising Bureau (IAB), which championed and authored the industry standards for counting ad impressions, also launched an initiative to "create a set of Click Measurement Guidelines." Clearly, loss of marketer and advertiser confidence in the validity of clicks and concerns about the scope of the click fraud problem were major catalysts in moving this project forward. The reality is the IAB committees, including the Search Engine Committee (of which I'm a member), have been discussing the need for clarity

> The crux of the click fraud issue is marketers shouldn't have to pay for clicks that aren't authentic or valid.

in click auditing, reconciliation, measurement, and definitions for some time.

No doubt Google, Yahoo!, Microsoft, Ask, and the other search engines have learned more about both advertiser perception of the click fraud issue and the confusion in the marketplace brought about by lawsuits and an explosion of companies offering pure click fraud monitoring solutions. All the major engines are big supporters of the IAB Click Measurement Working Group, as are the third-party ad-serving, click-counting, and campaign management companies. Impression fraud and the fuzzy way impressions were sometimes counted nearly derailed the online advertising business in its first decade. Similarly, click quality and click measurement standards are required to ensure all parties engaged in SEM are on the same page (pun intended).

Google even went so far as to start showing advertisers the valid and invalid clicks in AdWords reporting. It released a white paper (more of a research report) criticizing many players in the click fraud monitoring business and click fraud consultants for making fundamental analysis errors, resulting in an overstatement of the click fraud problem. The report even named companies whose estimates Google claims are flawed.

Interestingly, some of the report's points will be the same issues Fair Isaac will have to reconcile when reviewing participant data. The biggest issues are undifferentiated visits and use of log files as a data source when counting inbound clicks. We have found that inbound ad click redirects are the most accurate method for counting clicks and know their source and frequency. Clearly, Google isn't planning to issue credits to advertisers based on analyses it considers flawed.

In conclusion, perhaps I can start a dialogue on what exactly a billable click is. I don't expect this Truth to serve as an agenda point for any of the initiatives already underway or new ones that might be beginning. This is more stream of consciousness. Let's start by listing the elements all parties can likely agree define an advertising click, as follows:

> We have found that inbound ad click redirects are the most accurate method for counting clicks....

- A click is generated by a human person, not a robot or automated spider.
- When a human creates a click, she does so consciously and with purpose.
- Humans who click are interested in navigating to a specific page or site.
- Humans understand that clicking is a navigational action resulting in the browser loading the new page or site. More nebulous areas relate to when a human-generated click with all the preceding intentions shouldn't be billable. Should a click be billable if

  - The person repeats the navigational behavior on the same exact page (SERP), resulting in a second click within a session or short period?

  - The person clicks a link to the same advertiser on a different SERP or from a different contextual or behavioral ad impression?

  - The person is the advertiser's competitor and doesn't have a genuine interest in the ad?

If any of the preceding or other conditions invalidate a click, does the publisher, network, third party, or advertiser have the responsibility to reconcile the billable and invalid clicks? My guess is much of the work done by the IAB in defining and standardizing impressions will be quite valuable in guiding the next round of standards-setting.

Stay tuned. This discussion is far from over.

TRUTH

29

Broad match keywords

Think you only get traffic on the keywords you buy? Buying traffic based on keywords is simple, right? You pick the keywords you have an interest in and that's the traffic you get to your site, right? WRONG. Unless you specify otherwise, most engines use broad match as the default when you set up your campaign. You might think you know what broad match is and the kinds of keywords that trigger your ad being shown (and therefore cost you money) when searchers select your ad. You might be in for a broad match surprise, which might include misspellings, synonyms that are not as similar as you might prefer, and even typographical errors on domain names (both your own and those of the competition). For the scoop on exactly how and why you have to monitor and tune your broad match listings, read on.

> Unless you specify otherwise, most engines use broad match as the default when you set up your campaign.

The first manifestation of a broad match, which still impacts you today, was actually present before Google even launched CPC AdWords. Overture, the precursor to Yahoo! Search Marketing, added such a "feature" to its listings in 2000. That feature was named Match Driver and was not something you could turn on or off through the Direct Traffic Center (DTC) console used to configure campaigns. Match Driver was originally described as a feature that "takes misspellings, hyphenated terms, compound words, singular/plural combinations, and punctuation variations of most popular terms and maps them to the most common form of that term. Let's say that a consumer searched on the term "e commerce." Match Driver would match "e commerce" with all the permutations of that term, such as "e-commerce," "e comerce," and "e-comerce," to the primary form, "ecommerce," and display the same set of results. This tool helps consumers find what they're looking for on the Internet, which enhances our search engine and allows us [Overture] to drive even more traffic to our advertisers' sites."

Yahoo! updated the description recently, and it is available at http://searchmarketing.yahoo.com/en_HK/rc/srch/dtcfaq_mt.php.

Notice that in addition to the revised Match Driver definition, Yahoo! also includes information on its enhanced matching program. With enhanced match, Yahoo! has yet another way to match your listings with the searcher's activities while preserving (at least in theory) the searcher's intent. Yahoo!'s enhanced matching makes use of titles and descriptions, as well as the search keywords you specify in the DTC. The net result of these features is that you might be getting traffic for keywords you didn't expect. As long as both the searcher intent and the conversion/ROI is still there, and your spending on the unexpected keyword clicks isn't very high in comparison to your campaign's total spend, you probably won't worry and perhaps even ignore the issue. However, unless you know what to look for, you might not even realize you have a problem.

Yahoo! also has, as mentioned earlier, an advanced match option that is voluntary, and in this case, you have the option to use negative keywords to control the cases where your ad is chosen for display. This makes adjustment of keyword mix much easier, but monitoring in Yahoo! is still important.

> Google also tries to match your ads to user intent even if the match is a bit beyond what you might have expected.

Google also tries to match your ads to user intent even if the match is a bit beyond what you might have expected. Google's extended broad match includes misspellings, and synonyms, and most surprisingly, it often includes typos of domain names. The net result from this is that you must monitor and tune your Google campaigns that include broad match listings (which, of course, you should use strategically, but not exclusively). The best solutions to monitor your actual keyword traffic flowing from paid listings will be either high-end campaign management platforms and tools that can report the difference between the keyword bid upon and the search keyword, or web analytics systems and tools.

Monitoring isn't enough. When appropriate, use negative keywords to eliminate your ads showing for a search. If the engine's system doesn't allow for a matching system to be turned off, and you believe that your ad is being shown for irrelevant queries, I'm sure that at least some people at the search engine would like to know, even if your rep isn't particularly enthusiastic about passing on the data you gathered about conversion rates.

From the consumer perspective, sometimes the extended broad match in Google or the Match Driver and enhanced matching are highly relevant; other times, the systems fail for both the consumer and the marketer, but are close enough that the searcher clicks on your ad anyway, costing you money.

So, although broad match is a powerful tool, the engines' definitions of broad match are getting broader all the time in an attempt to make more money while still preserving relevance. Just remember that although relevance might be enough for the search engine, you might also demand profit. That's why you or your search agency must be monitoring, measuring, and tuning your listings as needed.

TRUTH

30

PPC backward and forward

Traditional web analytics might give you the wrong signals, steering you to the wrong decisions about your PPC search campaigns. The mere fact that a search term was popular a month, week, or even a day ago does not ensure any continued currency in the public mind. Unfortunately, most marketers' decisions about marketing PPC and other on- and offline marketing campaigns are based purely on historical data. That's like driving in a race using an oversized rearview mirror. Sure, your mirror will tell you a little about the curves in the road and traffic's general position, but trying to drive competitively at high speed while looking behind is a formula for disaster.

My team and I have found that building on campaign data and overlaying marketing objectives results in a forward-thinking plan with a good chance of hitting these future objectives instead of getting mired in a scenario where positive change seems nearly impossible.

Yet web analytics companies, ad-tracking systems, engine-based analytics, and campaign management systems place a huge emphasis on what happened in the past. Fancy, high-sizzle interfaces reveal tons of information about keyword-level detail regarding CTR, conversion rate, and possibly revenue, profit margin, and whether the customer is new or returning.

...most marketers' decisions about marketing PPC and other on- and offline marketing campaigns are based purely on historical data.

To win the race, in addition to looking forward at your objective, you must know who's next to you, especially in a heavy competition. In the competitive PPC environment, those next to you are bidders who in real time are sometimes ahead of you and sometimes behind. These bidders have a greater impact on your success than how your ad performed in the past.

No one can argue that a lot can be gleaned from prior data, particularly if data is analyzed on a macro level as well as on a keyword-by-keyword basis. Some bid management systems even draw analogies to how analytics from the stock market play a role in decision making. Unfortunately, like mutual finds and stocks, there's a limit to how predictive a model can be using purely archival historical information.

Indeed, historical data is a campaign strategy's foundation. But to truly win in an auction market, one must factor in real-time data and plan experiments that allow one to maneuver quickly as the marketplace changes. This requires testing and probing the markets for elasticity on high-volume keywords. This elasticity testing can be performed automated, manually, or by using some combination of both methods.

Don't fixate on the bids

Take a deep breath and remember what the bid is designed to accomplish. Higher bids are means to ends that include greater visibility, more clicks, and more business. But ROI, profit, and other success metrics restrain us from bidding to higher positions within our bid management systems. We fight with other marketers whose bids might be higher or lower than ours (given relative quality scores), regardless of whether these competitors are bidding rationally or not. Our objective is to determine how to raise our reserve price or otherwise give us an edge. Instead of fixating on the bids, we need to set an objective of raising our reserve price through conversion improvements or revenue/profitability improvements.

Enhance conversion rates

Use the data you have to plan a roadmap showing exactly how much lift in conversion rate you'll require to make a material change in position over time. For example, the results of your elasticity testing might indicate that a 32% increase in CPC is required to jump two positions in the SERP. To keep ROI constant, you need to figure out how to raise conversion rates by 32%. Of course, the difference in lead or order volume produced by your listing being two positions higher in the SERP will be fairly dramatic, often double or more (particularly if you move from the right rail to the top). However, be sure to vigorously monitor conversion rates, because a jump to first position will sometimes reduce the rate. You might think that increasing your conversion rate by 32% would be challenging; yet a conversion lift from 3% to 3.96% will get you there. If you can't find this kind of lift anywhere in your campaign, look at clusters where conversion is already there by geo or day-part.

Enhance revenue and profit

Conversion rate isn't your only leverage to a higher position. Profit or revenue enhancement works as well. Revenue enhancement can be driven by doing such simple things as changing your promotions. For instance, instead of offering free shipping at $50, make it free at $59 or $65. The average order size might jump, giving you immediate leverage in your bidding strategy. Once again, if you can't raise your revenue across the entire clickstream on high-potential keywords, consider a segmentation analysis.

TRUTH

31

In-house versus outsourced SEM: The CMO's guide to the outsourcing debate

Should marketers manage search in-house or outsource it? Conference sessions are devoted to this question, research analysts weigh in about it during briefings, and white papers have delved into it. Some in the SEM agency community and some in-house SEM practitioners are engaged in a war of words over this point. Complicating the picture: campaign-enhancing technology, including bid management, landing-page testing, click segmentation systems, and supporting web analytics.

Perhaps each side is solidifying its career prospects. Reality lies far from the rhetoric presumably aimed at CMO, marketing VPs, and the executive suite in general. After all, the livelihood of both in-house and agency SEM practitioners depends on what the executive decision makers believe to be the optimal scheme.

What are the merits of outsourcing SEM compared to those of managing SEM (both PPC search and SEO) in-house? The answer depends on multiple factors that must be evaluated before selecting a strategy.

Even the definition of "outsourced SEM" can vary. For example, my team services some clients who believe they aren't outsourcing search because the partnership keeps certain roles and responsibilities on the client side, even though my team provides more than technology and tech support. Other clients receiving the same level of service consider such arrangements to be outsourcing. It's

> Some in the SEM agency community and some in-house SEM practitioners are engaged in a war of words over the insourced/ outsourced decision.

more important for marketing executives to determine the specific needs and campaign objectives, and then decide how best to achieve those goals.

The search marketing industry is barely a dozen years old. CMOs should consider other key business processes, such as legal and accounting functions, that are carried out in-house or by outside firms. Large corporations and even some midsize entities have in-house counsel but still rely on outside law firms, particularly when special external skills and knowledge best serve the enterprise. Likewise, managing accounting functions in-house doesn't preclude the use of an external accounting firm. Within marketing, the same continuum exists for traditional advertising and public relations.

A CMO must determine the balance of skills and expertise required to accomplish search marketing objectives. Such considerations might include whether to retain a combination of in-house staff and external expertise, such as production expertise, strategic experience, and analytical savvy.

As with legal and accounting services, an enterprise's SEM needs may change over time. When a major lawsuit looms, even a well-staffed in-house legal department will generally call in reinforcements from outside. Within media and search marketing, multiple factors influence the staff hours required to accomplish campaign objectives, including the following:

- A campaign's age
- A campaign's size, including engines, keywords, and segmentation groups
- Competitiveness of an industry segment
- Speed at which the search engines make changes to their offerings, including algorithms and types of media
- Frequency of change in product/service mix
- Seasonality of an industry
- Current employee team size
- Current employee team skills mix and level of experience
- Likelihood of employee turnover, which today is frequently driven by a shortage of SEM experience in the marketplace
- Changing technology needs
- Level of aggressiveness and willingness to test

At times in the campaign lifecycle, there might be significant opportunities that can only be captured by deploying significant production resources, uncovering knowledge through careful statistical analysis, or applying expertise. To build an in-house team for every stage of a campaign isn't optimal. Even the staunchest in-house SEM advocate, then, might miss huge opportunities and should consider a partnership during any mission-critical campaign.

123

Within paid search, exchange-traded (auctioned) media presents another important factor in determining the enabling technology's fit. Technology decisions occur within a "build versus buy" continuum, as do the services and expertise side of search. Technology can do more than automate mundane aspects of real-time auction media marketplaces. In some cases, it can be more effective than human effort alone. Yet technology poses challenges depending on the amount of customization and training required.

One challenge is the technology's level of customizability. Generally, the more customizable any technology is, the more powerful it is, but realizing this power often correlates with very high levels of training. Therefore, the level of support from your technology vendor is particularly important. Bells and whistles you'll never use are worse than worthless and clutter the user experience.

Bells and whistles you'll never use are worse than worthless and clutter the user experience.

If you're a CMO or other senior executive overseeing search marketing, consider the point on the continuum between in-house and outsourced that will best serve your organization now and for the next 6 to 12 months. Then revisit this mix if you determine that you're either missing profit/ growth opportunities or overspending on services for your current needs.

TRUTH

32

PPC search:
Create, influence, capture, and harvest demand

Search marketing has evolved, and the time is right for marketers to move beyond harvesting demand generated elsewhere by other media. Capturing and harvesting consumer or business demand already in play is easy and can be done passably using rudimentary web analytics or campaign management technology. Instead of being demand harvesters, marketers (those with brand budgets, in particular) must use search the same way they do other media: to influence consumers positively toward eventual purchase and create new demand for the brand and perhaps for their industry category as a whole.

Much of the traditional advertising we experience alerts us to a problem we didn't know we had or increases our awareness of the severity of a problem we have. Perhaps the ad is simply trying to convince us that we should take action to avoid a potential problem, such as wrinkled skin, a home burglary, ownership of a crappy car, or a dull Saturday night. Advertising often tells a story that provides a solution to that problem. And most advertising is designed to create demand, influence existing demand for a particular brand choice, harness that demand into action (by enhancing purchase intent), and then enable the retailer or other fulfiller to harvest that demand.

Most marketers have done a great job of harvesting customers from the clickstream driven from search impressions. Those search impressions and their resulting clicks don't just happen spontaneously; they're the result of media, advertising, marketing, buzz, store visits, news, or something in

> Remember: It's not just your own marketing or PR activities that stimulate search behavior.

the searcher's life that stimulated a search. Perhaps the searcher's coffeemaker broke that morning, or perhaps another medium was involved. Remember: It's not just your own marketing or PR activities that stimulate search behavior. Search behavior occurs at a macro level as a consequential result of all the activities, information, and communication a consumer touches or is touched by. That's why search marketers must be aware of the overall consumer response ecosystem.

Most SEM campaigns are primarily directed at harvesting demand. Don't get me wrong: Harvesting demand generated through other means is a great business, but it doesn't fully maximize the marketing opportunity we have in front of us. Search, paid search in particular, has inserted itself into the last step of the consumer purchasing process only recently, and some marketers consider any paid search dollars spent on brand terms to be a toll the search engine charges marketers. It's easy to see why one would adopt that mentality. Some marketers actually empower or permit affiliates to harvest customers for them. As marketers and advertisers, however, we need to look at the overall process of taking our customers through the buying cycle.

As more keyword-driven inventory becomes available, marketers will have an ongoing opportunity to revisit their media effectiveness criteria and definitions of success to facilitate the kinds of marketing and media decisions that create demand, influence individual buyer decisions, and help harness recently created demand.

For PPC search and contextual media, marketers must develop proxy metrics for the brand lift, purchase intent lift, and overall brand favorability that occur, not so much from the PPC search impression, but from the user clicking through and interacting with the site. This metric will vary among marketers, and some have postulated that pageviews or time onsite are great engagement indicators that should be used. These metrics shouldn't be used in a vacuum, however, particularly when data can be collected to determine if there's been a holistic impact on the overall segment of consumers touched by a campaign.

When expanding the list of post-click behaviors considered instrumental in the creation or influence on consumer demand, the marketing team must take into account more than just the keyword. Keywords might be an indicator of consumer intent, but they don't tell us much more about the consumer. The consumer audience we can target in PPC search, and particularly

> Keywords might be an indicator of consumer intent, but they don't tell us much more about the consumer.

in contextual and behavioral media, can be selected based on many of a media buyer's tried-and-true targeting options: age, gender, geography, day-part, and so on.

Microsoft's adCenter was the first platform to allow for incremental targeting by age and gender, but Google recently added age and gender targeting for listings across its extensive content network. When setting up campaigns, you'll now have a combination of data to validate and improve a campaign, as well as the application of targeting variables that have already proven to beat a run-of-network mix.

As more marketers take a holistic approach to buying PPC search and media, we might see a steady escalation in keyword prices, particularly in specific segments. So, if you see your position dropping, it might not be a crazy competitor bidding irrationally. It might be an extremely smart, forward-thinking rival, and you must be prepared to match his/her savvy and expertise.

TRUTH

33

Moving beyond campaign efficiency to campaign effectiveness

It's natural, especially in tough economic times, for marketers to focus on efficiency, and there's no more efficient marketing medium than PPC search. But if you focus purely on efficiency (perhaps because the campaign algorithms used by your technology provider are geared toward efficiency), you will miss a huge opportunity in search. And you can't afford to miss opportunities in any economic climate.

In PPC search, many people see efficiency as the process of maximizing the yield of a paid-placement campaign by adjusting all the variables the engine provides, either through the API or through a web-based interface. Don't get me wrong: Efficiency is good. But to thrive in any economic climate, one must combine efficiency with strategic testing to obtain effectiveness. Efficiency-focused tactics eliminate waste in a campaign based on the data and analytics available. However, it's impossible to find new opportunities if the data upon which you base your decisions is exclusively historical. The PPC market is dynamic and is characterized by price elasticity and keyword volatility. Throw in algorithmic changes, and you can't win by focusing purely on efficiency.

Unfortunately, many initiatives and strategies that take your campaign beyond efficiency to increased effectiveness (as measured by sales, profit, lead volume, or whatever your success metric) require a combination of tactics and strategy that is human resources-intensive. This is one reason why using technology alone, without incorporating an appropriate level of human analysis, often results in a stagnant campaign. Analysts need to make recommendations based on prior experience with respect to breaking out of the performance plateau.

> ...you can't win by focusing purely on efficiency.

Moving toward effectiveness

- **Retest ad creative**—Perhaps you have a particular creative in place now that has won the CTR and conversion rate shootout against other ad creative. That's great, but let's remember: That was then; this is now. The seasons have changed, your competitors are likely using new ad creative now, and perhaps what worked before is no longer the optimal creative. I've seen many cases (particularly involving power keywords, which drive the lion's share of any marketer's business) where advertisers gravitate toward a Dynamic Keyword Insertion (DKI)-style creative where the search keyword itself occupies most or all of the ad's title and is repeated in a boilerplate manner in the description as well. It's not unusual to search and find all three top paid listings with nearly identical creative. How can one expect to stand out amid this look-alike copy? Make sure you play around with enough variations to break out of the pattern while maintaining high relevance, CTR, and Quality Score. Are you including your URL in your creative tests? URLs are boldfaced by some of the engines when a portion of the URL matches the search query. Consider using subdirectories and subdomains (prefixes) in your display URL. A lift of a few tenths of a percent in CTR can make a difference in both position and your billed CPC, due to the influence of hybrid auctions and Google's Quality Score.

- **Use both singulars and plurals**—Hypothetically, most engines will broad match to and from plurals, but I've seen many instances when this wasn't the case. Even if it were, there's a compelling reason to have both variants in your campaign, especially in Google. All the engines display the searched keyword in titles and descriptions. Google, however, doesn't consistently boldface the plural when you search on the singular (although it often does). Microsoft's Live search (formerly MSN) doesn't boldface in either direction with singular or plural. So if you've used one option in your ad and the search is on the other option, you won't show up boldfaced. I've also seen instances where the Quality Score of ads goes up when singular and plural listings are separated and individually placed in a campaign. One can also argue that for many products, the user intent for singulars and plurals is actually different. Thus, a different user experience on the landing page might be appropriate to maximize conversions.

- **Test landing pages and personalization features**—We've all been testing landing pages for many years, but optimal landing pages change over time, just as creative does. Plus, it isn't clear that the same landing page is appropriate for all engines using

131

A small lift in overall conversion rate on the landing page generates a huge lift in the allowable CPC you can pay....

the same keyword. One can even do more sophisticated landing-page personalization using a variety of methods, technologies, and tools. A small lift in overall conversion rate on the landing page generates a huge lift in the allowable CPC you can pay while maintaining an optimal ROI.

There are many more things to test and change to improve a campaign and leverage into higher potential bids, which will secure higher positions resulting in more qualified traffic. To maximize the opportunity in search and auction media, take your mindset beyond campaign efficiency and look beyond the status quo. Change the rules of the game by manipulating other variables under your control, never stop testing, and you'll be on the road to true search campaign effectiveness.

TRUTH

34

Keyword testing and expansion done right

Keyword expansion gets a lot of attention. If you find a new keyword, and it can deliver significant incremental high-quality traffic to your site, your business will benefit for as long as it remains a profitable part of your overall campaign. There are right and wrong ways to add keywords to a campaign, however, because every keyword, new or old, must be tested to determine if it can become an important profit driver for your business.

Keyword discovery

Spider-based keyword extraction tools have been around for a while and can be used to generate keywords from your site. The less conventional use of these tools is to send the spider through your competitors' sites, one by one. Clearly the more accurate, usable list is the one your site generates. But depending on how closely your business matches that of your competitors, their lists may be useful. The quality of spider-generated lists is particularly high if the sites (yours or theirs) have good SEO. Remember to take trademark ownership into consideration when considering keyword use and be sure to follow keyword use editorial guidelines.

Any list you generate should be reevaluated in respect to stemming (plurals and other forms of the word), although many engines automatically expand searches to include stemmed versions of the keyword (in both organic/algorithmic results and paid listings). The closest match is generally considered most relevant, and the search engine puts only the exact match in boldface. Bolded keywords in titles and descriptions increase visibility and CTR, which is increasingly important in all engines.

Keyword implementation

Regardless of where new keyword suggestions originated, those keywords must be rolled into your campaign in a structured, intelligent way. Otherwise, you will do a ton of work without maximizing the opportunities inherent in the new keywords. After deciding a keyword or keyword phrase is worth testing, you must decide on campaign structure, a very different decision in each of the major engines.

Many of the new keywords you'll add will be phrases (if it's a mature campaign being expanded). Thus, there might be a compelling reason to use an AdGroup that contains similar phrases or root words. To determine if a phrase or word deserves that level of attention, I look at the following factors:

- **Search impression volume**—The minimum will vary by industry or client and has more to do with the rest of the campaign and the customer's potential importance than any arbitrary number. I might not recommend a custom AdGroup for a dating site when a phrase gets only 50 searches per month, for example. But for a site that sells music equipment, I might recommend a custom listing for the phrase "marshall ms2 practice amp," which probably gets about 100 searches per month across the major engines. A searcher seeing a custom-written ad for the item he seeks is very likely to respond.
- **Customer's importance**—If a business-to-business client sells "double-beam spectrophotometers," I don't care if that search term gets well under 100 searches per month. The searcher needs to understand the advertiser has what she seeks. A custom-written ad accomplishes this objective more effectively than a generic one.
- **Resources**—If you have internal or SEM agency resources available to implement best practices, take advantage of them. Alternatively, if you're resource-constrained and must concentrate on how to get your campaign's core keywords as efficiently as possible, temporary shortcuts on keyword expansion make sense.

Selecting landing pages

Regardless of whether you plan a sophisticated landing page test, you clearly have to start somewhere. Often, the winning landing pages for new keywords are the ones that currently win for you. So, compare the new keywords to those in your current campaign and imagine the searcher's intent.

Where to start a bid

Once your keywords are uploaded into an existing or new campaign structure, you must decide where to start bidding. Each keyword must have a bid range that meets your overall visibility, ROI, and long-term profit objectives. Your objective should be to bid as high as possible (given a specific ROI objective) to answer the question: "Will this keyword work for me?" Bidding too low has several negative side effects, including the following:

- A low number of clicks per day means you must wait a long time for sufficient data to accrue.
- It's easier to convince the engines that use hybrid algorithms that your ads are relevant if you get a high CTR early on. (This shouldn't happen, but it seems to.)
- Conversion rates might be lower at the lower positions.

Look at your current campaigns and the CPCs you pay for similar keywords. Boost those CPCs as much as you think you can based on potential increases in conversion rate. Regardless of your bid strategy, testing new keywords is an investment. It might require significant monetary investment before you find the winners and weed out the losers.

Data scarcity: Clustering by keyword stem and landing page

Keyword expansions often occur in the tail of the search distribution curve, meaning the keywords and phrases aren't often searched. Given a CTR of 2–15% and a conversion rate of 3–5% (both aggressive estimates), it would take years to know if a keyword resulted in profitable sales. Data modeling can help. Cluster keywords by stem (root word) or landing page. The data you get by looking at the cluster isn't perfect, but sometimes it's the best you've got.

When Keywords fail

You tried a keyword. The data look bad and the target ROI isn't likely to be met, even at lower bids/positions. Do you toss it? Perhaps, but before you discard that keyword, look carefully at the ad and the landing page. A mismatch or any other factor that provides a poor user experience can sabotage a perfectly good keyword.

TRUTH

35

Test or die:
Tune your Google ad
campaign

We can all learn from direct marketers. They've dealt with ROI-based marketing for years. Old-school catalogers might not yet grasp all the nuances of search engine marketing (SEM), but they do deal daily with maximizing ROI and profit from scarce resources (external mailing lists or internal customer lists). Catalog marketers deal with the scarcity of valuable customer lists or rental lists through testing. They always test new lists, new creative, new prices, and new offers. Several catalog marketers shared with me recently that, depending on the season, they might allocate anywhere from 10 to 45% of their media and creative budgets to tests.

It might seem like a risk to allocate more than 15% of a budget to testing, but catalog marketers know the biggest risk might be not testing at all. One catalog marketer emphasized this point by sharing his "test or die" credo with me. He means if he weren't constantly testing new things, his business would die a slow, steady death. This truth puts a new face on the importance of testing, and it inspired this Truth.

The same analogy holds true for search marketers. In PPC search, it might hold even truer because PPC prices continue a steady upward spiral. Keywords you could afford top position on yesterday might cost more today. You won't hit ROI targets unless you find a more efficient way to use those clicks, or a way to buy those clicks more cheaply. The only way to buy the same clicks for less is to get your CTR up to a higher percentage (resulting in a better AdRank/higher effective CPM for Google and the other search engines, which all use a "hybrid-auction" system rewarding high click volume).

Catalog marketers like the analogy of the psychic mailman I discussed in Truth 2, "Intrusive media versus the psychic postal carrier." He waits outside the doors of your best customers' homes. He has thousands of special product or service offers and is poised to ring the doorbell only at the moment buyers start thinking about a specific product or need. If a

> You won't hit ROI targets unless you find a more efficient way to use those clicks, or a way to buy those clicks more cheaply.

customer began thinking about a new down ski parka, the psychic mailman would tear out the appropriate page from a catalog and hand it over.

Imagine if there were three or four different pages in that catalog that might work. A truly psychic mailman could pick the best pages to present.

Search marketing keyword placements are an investment. Past performance can help predict future results, but results can't be predicted too far into the future.

Be sure to structure tests to provide the highest possible profit lift. The most common test is adding new keywords or engines to your campaign. The best way to test campaigns with new keywords or new search engines is to make a best guess as to copy, landing page, and offer to get a baseline. You can do so quickly by starting at the top of search results (paying more for the fast data), or you can take a more moderate approach. Just because a keyword doesn't hit your ROI target the first time doesn't mean you should bid low or trash it entirely.

First ask the following:

■ Does your business experience seasonality that could change conversion rates?
■ Did you try the best landing page?
■ Was copy written for the prospects and their state of mind?
■ What was your competition doing at the time?
■ Have you changed pricing?
■ Has marketplace pricing for your product changed?
■ Are you or your competition currently getting lots of PR or spending heavily in other media?
■ Will your conversion rate change as you change position based on the search engine's syndication network?

Tests you want to make include the following:

■ **Keyword expansion**—The most commonly recommended engine-side experiment is keyword expansion. Yes, keyword expansion is an experiment. Some keywords will work well, and others will fail.

- **Creative testing on power keywords**—All engines now reward a high-predicted CTR. If the engines think your ad will be well clicked, they'll let it appear at a higher position, without a higher bid cost.
- **Campaign reorganization**—Campaign reorganization is another often-overlooked test. It may be as simple as moving keywords out of ad groups that contain too many unrelated words.
- **Landing page testing**—Landing page testing and tuning is the most popular site-side testing, and with good reason: A poor landing page experience can cause the site visitor to use the dreaded Back button.
- **Offer testing**—Offer testing is an offshoot of landing page testing that relates specifically to the offers you provide on the landing page.
- **Technology enhancements**—Every month, there are seemingly more technology enhancements you can bolt onto a site or use to handle clicks. Based on tests from my internal teams, some of the latest enhancements show significant promise.

You can test many campaign elements continuously. There are now opportunities to test even more variables based on demographic, psychographic, and other data providing advanced targeting options. These options add important dimensions to your campaign that extend beyond which keywords users searched before arriving at your site.

So remember: Test or die. A final point: In cases where you're working with an agency, many of these tests require coordinating the agency and in-house teams. Make sure everyone brings unique expertise and knowledge to the testing process for the best results.

TRUTH

36

Best practices for PPC: Capturing the search curve tail

A search curve is a graphical representation of the number of times a given query is searched within a given period. A curve's tail is amazingly long and flat. These unique searches can be difficult to predict with certainty, but online tools provide a reasonable basis for researching how the search curve looks for your business during each season. Before Yahoo! went to a hybrid-auction model, its keyword selection tool enabled search marketers to easily inspect the search curve tail; unfortunately, it's no longer available.

Consider the keyword "MP3," a generic term with millions of searches each day. This term doesn't reveal whether the searcher wants MP3s or an MP3 player. Farther down the curve, only a handful of people search "free online mp3 music download," a much more specific query. Clearly, the tail is quite long, meaning that some very diverse, unique searches occur every day.

Your true reserve price on a bid should reflect the click's value....

The key to strategically capturing the search curve tail lies in the following best practices:

- Determine when to alter copy for different searches that share a similar intent.
- Identify the best structure to tune copy and landing pages as you move from generics to specifics.
- Use tracking, metrics, and strategy to determine the best bids for each point down the search curve, including accounting for positive user behaviors that will eventually result in sales and (more importantly) profit.
- Know when to use additional features, such as Google's ad Dynamic Keyword Insertion (DKI).

Let's cover the copy-tuning process. Tuning copy is labor-intensive, so you don't want to do it unless there's a reasonable chance the investment will pay off, particularly if you should consider other, higher return on investment (ROI) activities. Depending on the lead's or sale's value, you might want to continue tuning the ad copy and message so it more closely matches the intent expressed by queries that occur much farther down the tail.

Use your true reserve bid price, along with conversion rate, combined with the projected keyword search volume, as indicators of importance. Your true reserve price on a bid should reflect the click's value (even if the current

By re-categorizing a Google campaign, you can get the same click for less cash....

bid is much less). This way, you can tune ad copy from the areas of highest opportunity first, and then move down.

Google's broad match feature is an easy way to cast a wide net; broad match (discussed in Truth 30, "PPC backward and forward") delivers clicks on a basket of terms. But broad match isn't the most effective way to efficiently reach the tail. Instead, break out the most important phrases into new AdGroups when landing pages and creative could be improved for those searches. By re-categorizing a Google campaign, you can get the same click for less cash because the tuned creative in a new AdGroup often gets a higher AdRank (after an initial testing period to determine your ad's AdRank).

Yahoo! also has an advanced match type, but it's far better to think of words that might be searched and bid on them separately. Exact match always trumps advanced match in terms of securing a higher position on a SERP.

Use tracking data to develop a campaign that doesn't focus myopically on immediate conversion. All advertising has the potential to influence future purchase behavior. Not being there to influence later on- or offline behavior isn't optimal. Use whatever on- or offline data you have to understand how search influences behavior at every stage of the buying process. Know how your site fits into that process, too.

Engines, including Google, are rolling out campaign settings specifically designed to help marketers reach further down the tail. Google's DKI feature works very well for short queries but loses effectiveness for long searches due to limited space.

Millions of searchers use millions of unique search phrases to find what they want. Capitalize on their needs and behaviors as they create the tail of the search distribution, or your competition will beat you to it.

Although the "long tail" of search is important, don't forget to look at additional targeting methods that can slice and dice the traffic in the search distribution head in new ways. Power keywords are those popular keywords that might occur early in the research stages of many consumers' decision-making processes, but a big chunk of these consumers might be ready to buy or close to it. By analyzing post-click behavior of visitors using these power keywords, we can intelligently create our own tail and, therefore, improve our chances of capturing the searchers who are of greatest value to our businesses. We can create several obvious tails, but we must keep segmentation analysis balanced between reach/scale and improved targeting:

- **Geography**—With the launch of Yahoo!'s Panama in 2006, all three major search engines now enable us to set up campaigns specifically targeting geographical segments. Google even gives us additional screen real estate (on the right rail only) if the ad is geographically targeted. After looking at geographic data sets, I've found that segmenting at the designated market area (DMA) level is better for most clients than segmenting at the state level. However, look at your data to determine what's best for you. Although zip code or radius-level targeting is available from most providers, you'll have to decide how far out in the geographic tail you want to venture.

- **Day-part**—Searchers for your product or service might be very different people at different times of day. If you can segment your day-parts and personalize for them, you've created another tail.

- **Demographic segments**—Microsoft's system enables us to create a tail based on age and gender, which could provide particularly important targeting variables for your business. Age and gender alone can result in significant additional permutations you can use in your campaign structure. Do the analyses on your business to see if creating an age and gender tail makes sense for you.

TRUTH

37

Improve site usability to enhance conversion rates

Is your site meeting searchers' needs? Have you segmented your search campaigns based on the predictable needs or profiles of searchers and their buying-cycle stages? Your site needn't be poorly designed or have shoddy usability to benefit tremendously from a bit of help. Any site that's less than optimal for any major segment of a search campaign results in a mediocre campaign; non-optimal conversion rates can prohibit it from reaching marketing objectives.

Conversion improvement and usability enhancement have nothing to do with having an award-winning site. Even a snazzy, flashy site, designed by the hottest agency, might have far to go for optimal conversion enhancement. A site can be great in many ways and still not reach optimal levels of conversion and efficiency.

> A site can be great in many ways and still not reach optimal levels of conversion and efficiency.

One thing I'm very disappointed in is many "top" web development firms don't understand or embrace usability and conversion marketing. Macromedia's Flash, for example, is a powerful tool in the web developer arsenal, but it isn't the answer to all design challenges. Design and development agency staffs are trained in Flash but not in organic SEO best practices. Nor do they understand how to read a creative brief that includes usability parameters and user objectives to meet marketing objectives.

Of course, the account teams at these agencies might not generate full creative briefs that include strategy and objectives as well as design preferences (color, tone, resolution, fonts, copy, and so on). Perhaps the media teams at these agencies don't realize their jobs don't stop at buying and trafficking media.

A media team can be a catalyst for change at an agency while increasing billings and making clients happier. Can you guess what happens to media spend when site efficiency and conversion goes up? Spending rises accordingly, particularly in paid-placement search, where conversion rates might have throttled the spending on power keywords driving the bulk of your sales. Improved conversion rates can mean keywords that were too pricey for a top-four position suddenly become affordable. The result can be an increase in visitors that is orders of magnitude greater than that produced by lower-tier listings.

> Improved conversion rates can mean keywords that were too pricey for a top-four position suddenly become affordable.

The need for conversion marketing services is fueled by the relentless pressure of the PPC auction marketplace and the need to maximize return from affiliate marketing channels. Of course, all media benefit from improved site usability and conversion marketing best practices. Marketers likewise must pay attention when their agencies recommend usability enhancement projects and conversion marketing initiatives. No marketer likes to hear that the site he just spent tens or hundreds of thousands of dollars to build is crippling paid and organic SEM initiatives. Don't feel singled out if conversion marketing wasn't high on the list of priorities when your site was built. It's more than likely that some elements of your web site hold you back from the success you could achieve in paid search.

In the offline world of retail and catalog marketing, conversion marketing is practiced regularly and frequently. Perhaps interactive agencies and web design shops aren't the right organizations to help marketers overcome the challenges of a less-than-optimal site with less-than-optimal landing pages and user experience. Consultants and in-house designers might have an advantage in addressing this major problem.

> No marketer likes to hear that the site he just spent tens or hundreds of thousands of dollars to build is crippling paid and organic SEM initiatives.

Conversion improvements enable marketers to bid higher for the keywords and keyword phrases they need. If their keywords are already in top positions, conversion increases shoot profit and revenue straight to the bottom line.

I predict a renaissance in the web design and interactive agency industries, particularly in the sector of site redesign for maximum usability and optimal conversion. A driving force will be the Pay-Per-Click (PPC) search marketplace. To spend and grow campaigns in the PPC marketplaces at anywhere near a reasonable profit and volume, marketers need optimally performing sites for searchers.

TRUTH

38

Beaten at your own name:
Buying your brand

Are you getting beaten by your own name? Buying your own brands and trademarks in PPC search can present a serious strategic dilemma, particularly when that brand as a keyword ranks number one in organic search. This is something mega-marketer Procter & Gamble faces with one of its largest brands, Head & Shoulders shampoo. Searchers using this term will see several organic listings (one from P&G's international site, another from a U.S.-based site, and a listing from Wikipedia). I'm sure that P&G would rather have searchers go to the site most likely to persuade searchers of Head & Shoulders' virtues, but by relying on an organic-only strategy, it cedes this all-important decision to Google, Yahoo!, and Microsoft.

All search engines recognize a site with sufficient quality content might deserve two organic result slots. This might also be the case for those who put time and energy into building sites to be search-engine friendly so that they are full of useful, relevant content.

When deciding between paid and organic, you can consider the situation as you might with real estate: More is better. Yet given a fixed budget, many marketers assume with one or two organic links, searchers will find those links and click. Those marketers prefer to allocate their search budget to generic or nonbranded product/ service keywords that describe either the problem solved or other relevant ideas. The thinking goes, "Better to spend money acquiring new customers who don't yet feel strongly enough about my brand to search for it by name."

Sometimes, that line of reasoning makes sense. But there are some critical issues to consider if you struggle with whether to buy your brand name in PPC search, as follows:

> When deciding between paid and organic, you can consider the situation as you might with real estate: More is better.

- **Does your competition buy your brand keyword?** If so, you risk losing customers who thought enough of your brand to actually search for it. That search might even have been the result of your on- or offline advertising that piqued curiosity.

150

- **Does your retail or reseller channel buy the brand keyword?** If so, it might seem like good news because you'll get the order through the channel. But if your resellers and retailers aren't in an exclusive relationship with you, you risk a cross-sell to the competition, even on your licensed retailer's site. This is very common in the travel business, where a searcher is indifferent to the subtleties between three hotel brands she considers a close match in amenities, service, and other attributes. One brand's search transforms into another brand's booking. The same could occur with Head & Shoulders if drugstore.com is a bidder in all three top PPC engines and enables visitors to link to the "Hair Care" category from the Head & Shoulders results page. Even a modest cross-sell makes sense for the merchant if it pays for the click.

> ...if your resellers and retailers aren't in an exclusive relationship with you, you risk a cross-sell to the competition, even on your licensed retailer's site.

- **Do your affiliates buy your brand keyword?** If you let your affiliates buy your brand keywords instead of buying them yourself, you give your affiliates a *huge* gift. Affiliates often make a five-to-one return on buying brand keywords. For every $5 you pay them, they pay only $1. Flip it around. You overpay by a factor of five for the orders or leads the affiliate generates.

- **Do you feel lucky or do you want control?** The search engine will pick a page to suggest to the searcher, use that HTML Title tag, and then select some copy from your body or description meta data. Is that the message you want people to see? Will the organic link's landing page provide the highest conversion? Subpar front- and back-end messaging can confuse a searcher or derail a sale. PPC listings help control at least one message and user experience invoked by the searcher by clicking on a listing.

- **Do you want to bifurcate your audience or engage in self-selection filtering?** People responding to and engaging with organic links might represent a discrete population from those selecting paid links. Similarly, different customer clusters might respond to promotional messaging versus educational messaging. With paid search's controllability, you can provide options so that people can self-select.

- **Is regional message control important?** PPC search provides a high level of geographic message control. Search is the first medium in which channel conflict is so pronounced that the conflict level often reaches across company departments and can involve regional aspects as well (due to distribution agreements).
- **Do you have a negativity problem?** Some brands have a problem with unhappy users posting poor reviews or even "sucks" pages. Paid listings appearing on top of the organic results can push negative pages lower on the results page.
- **Do you understand the interaction effects between organic and PPC?** Run simple cannibalization tests by pulse-testing your paid listings on brand terms. You measure the incremental cost of acquiring leads, clicks, and purchases through paid listings, even if there is some cannibalization of organic traffic. By focusing on the marginal ROI or profit, you can get a better handle on brand search's real value. Even a good pulse test measure of cannibalization doesn't always tell the whole story. The customer purchase cycle often includes two to six (or more) searches, according to a comScore/DoubleClick study. Paid and search clicks occur all the way through the decision process; some are paid, some are organic, but all might influence a final purchase. Consider a more in-depth test across organic and paid traffic to gain a better understanding of your brand name's incremental value as a search term.

Traffic from your brand keywords is the most valuable to you, the brand owner, but it's also valuable to your competition and reseller or retail channel. A person who types in a brand name is much more likely to know exactly what she wants, but she might be open to suggestion. Don't get beaten on your own name and lose this customer.

TRUTH

39

Brands, trademarks, and the brand marketer's dilemma

Should brand and direct marketers buy their own trademarks as keywords? Should you buy other competitive trademarks in your Google, Yahoo!, or other search campaigns? There are no simple answers, but the issue of trademarks as keywords persists as one of the most vexing issues in search marketing.

The GEICO versus Google lawsuit

The first major skirmish in what has become a continual battle over Google's trademark policy surfaced several years ago, when insurer GEICO sued Google for allowing GEICO's competitors to buy the keyword "GEICO" to serve ads for competing services. The issue was ultimately settled out of court, but the legal precedent was set, allowing Google to sell trademarked terms and allow marketers to run ads, so long as they don't include use of the trademark in the ad's actual copy. The settlement followed an earlier oral ruling asserting that only when a trademark appears in an ad keyed to the trademark as a search term is there potential trademark violation and consumer confusion. As Google's trademark policy has long been that marketers can't use a trademark to which they don't have ad copy rights, GEICO's PR mavens claimed victory. But the primary litigation objective—to stop the bidding—fell in Google's favor. Essentially, the judge upheld Google's policy of forbidding misleading trademark use in ad copy.

> ...the issue of trademarks as keywords persists as one of the most vexing issues in search marketing.

What is a trademark?

The U.S. patent and trademark office defines a trademark as "a word, phrase, symbol, or design, or a combination of words, phrases, symbols, or designs, that identifies and distinguishes the source of the goods of one party from those of others." Branded terms are typically trademarked, which means that they ordinarily cannot be used by competitors in marketing messages.

What is Google's trademark policy?

Google's policy on trademarks enables advertisers to use trademarked terms as keywords, although the GEICO lawsuit has caused it to restrict the appearance of competitors' names in the actual text ad. Still, giving competitors the right to bid on the trademarked term that a given company has spent millions (possibly hundreds of millions) of dollars establishing in the public mind is maddening

Google itself forbids anyone from bidding on any Google-branded terms, which further angers those claiming that their brands have been hijacked.

to these marks' owners, who consider it a form of "hijacking." Interestingly, Google itself forbids anyone from bidding on any Google-branded terms, which further angers those claiming that their brands have been hijacked.

What should marketers do?

If you own a branded search term, and competitors are using this term to trigger search ads, your options are limited. You can file a complaint through Google, but this in itself is unlikely to stop the practice, given that Google allows it. You can rely on your own organic listings, which if prominent enough, can stem the flow of traffic flowing to your competitors. Or you can buy your own branded terms, pay enough for them so that your paid listings are always top-ranked, and consider it a cost of doing business in the search economy. If you have

If you own a branded search term, and competitors are using this term to trigger search ads, your options are limited.

deep pockets, of course, you can sue Google, as many firms have done, and attempt to reach a settlement.

The battle over trademarked terms is ongoing, and perhaps someday there will be an authoritative legal ruling that establishes a rule—either pro or con—on Google's practices. But Google is likely to fight any push to do away with the current practice, because there is so much money at stake. In the meantime, the way things are provides both good news for marketers who seek to slipstream their marketing messages into the brand-seeking clickstream, and bad news for those who want to exclude searchers from considering alternative products or services.

TRUTH

40

Start at the ad: CTR improvement with better creative

They don't call ads "creative" for nothing. Better descriptions provide buyers with a better user experience. If more people who see your ads click on them, it's an immediate campaign volume multiplier. In Google, if new creative is more compelling and gets a higher CTR, you'll get more volume due to an increased conversion from impression to click and a higher position at the same CPC. Alternately, your current position might become less expensive due to the Google AdWords "bid x CTR" method of ranking ads in search results.

Use inverted pyramids

In journalistic writing, one starts with the conclusion, and then follows with the strongest statements supporting that conclusion. If an editor must cut, she can cut from the bottom without losing much impact. Similarly, a reader can come away with a solid idea of the story thesis from the first paragraph. Pay-Per-Click (PPC) search ads should also be top-loaded for immediate effect. Some venues that display PPC search results truncate listings. This means you might lose part of the title and description you just perfected.

Use dynamic keyword insertion

One important way to create better creative is to include each keyword in the ad creative. Google and other engines will boldface keywords in the search when they also appear in the creative. This increases visibility and CTR. Google has an automated method to enable you to have the searcher's keywords inserted into your ad (assuming the keyword string isn't too long to fit). The Dynamic Keyword Insertion (DKI) system uses a creative template and keeps all the other ad copy the same. Here is an example of Google's DKI formatting:

Title: {Keyword: Default creative} always here

In this example, "Keyword" is replaced by the actual search phrase or term. If the actual search is too long to fit in the title or description, the default is displayed in its place. Here, "Default creative" is displayed. Anything outside the squiggle brackets ("{}") is always displayed. In all cases, the words "always here" are in the title. So, if a user searched for "car," the result would be: "Car always here." Say the user searched for "New York state car marketplace pricing." The phrase is too long to be dynamically replaced, so the title would read: "Default creative always here."

The Google DKI feature can be used in the title or description. Generally, CTR increases with DKI over many other creative executions. For important Google keywords, using templates might not suffice to make creative as compelling and relevant as possible. Instead of using DKI alone, place keywords in AdGroups, where the message can be tuned to the specific offer or landing page. DKI is useful, but use it with discretion. Overusing DKI automatically inserts the searcher's exact query in the ad title. This results in ad homogeneity within the SERP's PPC portion. So to stand out, it might make sense to skip the DKI or to use the full search term in the title and use it creatively in the description instead.

Use compelling copy and offers

What do you have that your competition doesn't? Can you fit that unique, relevant, targeted benefit into 70 to 190 characters? If you want to drive sales or lead volume, a slightly more compelling offer might raise the CTR on your ad while maintaining clickstream quality. Every click to a relevant landing page reduces the chance your competition will get the click and make the sale (or get the lead).

When thinking about what offers might be attractive or how best to describe what you have to satisfy the searcher, don't think about what you like to see personally. You probably aren't in your target audience profile. Instead, put yourself in the mindset of your best prospective customer. What gets them excited?

Some of my clients have had dramatic success changing their copy to be more enticing. However, not every tactic is best for every marketer. That's why a testing regimen is critical. Don't start changing things without understanding your baseline. Always compare any new creative against current ads. Compare the CTR and watch for changes in conversion. That said, the following guidelines provide ways to make your ad copy more compelling:

- If you sell on price, put the price in the title.
- Put the price in the description; lead with it if it's important.
- Consider using a percentage off or a percentage savings message if you sell on price.

- Add "free shipping," but make sure your free shipping doesn't have strings.
- Use hot, power words that aren't superlatives, such as "great," "save," "savings," "shop," "huge," "latest," "excellent," "selection," "low," "discount," "cheap," "choose," "now," "wholesale," "special," "on sale," "compare," "massive," "experienced," "specializing," "deals," "leading," "VIP," "outstanding," "rebate," "coupon," "wonderful," "search," "stunning," "fabulous" (this one works better on some demographics), "detailed," "easy," "guaranteed," and "quality."
- Use brands in the copy if you carry them. If you're a brand, use that. A ton of money was spent building the brand. Use the brand equity to improve the copy.

Use enticing display URLs

If your URL is a well-known brand, you have an immediate advantage. This is one area where you see return on a branding investment. Searchers click on names they know and trust.

If you don't yet have a powerful brand, consider a micro-site, where the domain matches the target segment. You can use the micro-site just for paid search. With domains costing under $10 a year from many registrars, there isn't much of a hurdle in testing a unique URL that contains the keywords central to your business.

Use seasonal copy

If your business is seasonal, perhaps your creative should be, too. Should your message change during year-end holidays? Are there key messages you want to convey at different times of the year? By applying the guidelines we covered earlier to seasonal advertising and testing results, you'll know when to swap out the creative message.

TRUTH

41

Day-parts, day of the week, and other cherry-picking techniques

In radio, it's called drive time; in TV land, it's called prime time; in the wonderful world of SEM, it's called lunchtime. Day-parts are a way of segmenting media by the time of day, because viewer receptiveness to messages and readiness to take action varies based on the time of day. Even the retail business has day-parts—times of the day when customers are more valuable and more likely to buy.

It should come as little surprise, then, that certain search engine inventory can be bought by day-part. Day-parts are one way of selecting out the premium inventory and going beyond the average—potentially doubling your effective SEM marketing budget.

A significant percentage of SEM inventory is sold in auction-style environments. The auction environment might sometimes make your blood boil; however, there are positive aspects to it. The real-time nature of Yahoo! (formerly Overture), Google, and other Pay-Per-Click (PPC) auction engines provides the opportunity for savvy marketers to take advantage of the differences in searcher behavior at different times of day, by measuring post-click results.

Of course, the Internet is a national and global medium, and, therefore, times of day are relative—unlike radio or TV day-parting, where the exact time of day the audience is experiencing can be determined. Online marketers don't need to know exactly from where each searcher is originating, and even if they did, they can't target by

> In radio, it's called drive time; in TV land, it's called prime time; in the wonderful world of SEM, it's called lunchtime.

the click. All marketers really need to know is their conversion results and how the results vary by time of day.

The following are some questions to ask:

- When are the most orders coming in?
- When are the most profitable orders coming in?
- When are conversion rates the best?
- Are these patterns repeating day after day, week after week?

Although instituting a feedback loop will likely add significant efficiency to your campaign, you can take data analysis even further with day-parting. But you must understand how day-parts work for *your* site. Not every site can implement the same day-part strategy, because each site has a different target market and a different buying cycle. Business-to-business (B2B) marketers and business-to-consumer (B2C) marketers will have different day-part optimization opportunities. The B2B marketer might also have significant weekday-versus-weekend shifts in value.

Let's assume after gaining an understanding of the relative value of your keywords/listings in the various engines, you have your campaign humming along. With a feedback loop in place, your listings might even be adjusting based on time of day automatically if the volume of clicks in an hour is high. However, your heat-seeking missile tactic can be even more powerful if it knows where the target is going to be before it gets there.

Day-part analysis gives you a predictive model that enables you to modify your campaign for maximum day-part-derived power. You do this by collecting and analyzing data about conversion percentages. The most difficult part is deciding how granular you want to go. Most marketers will derive a large percentage of the day-part efficiency by looking at day-part conversion data on the aggregate (mixing keywords, engines, and products together).

As an example, let's imagine a catalog marketer on the U.S.'s East Coast that ships throughout the U.S. We'll call the company Yuppiemart, and we will look at the segment of its campaign where the target Cost-Per-Order (CPO) is $35. Much of the online shopping among the U.S. population goes on during lunch, and for Yuppiemart, the target market is likely to be employed. The Yuppiemart marketing VP is looking to optimize the campaign by conversion to sale, keeping the CPO under $35. (It would be possible to factor in catalog requests or phone inquiries from prospects not quite ready to buy, but let's take one optimization example at a time.)

Yuppiemart's conversion from click-through to sale is 4.5% from 11:30 a.m. to 5:30 p.m., 2.5% from 5:30 p.m. to 1:30 a.m., 2.0% from 1:30 a.m. to 7:30 p.m., and then back to 2.5% until the lunch crowd hits again. If you were to look at premium listings over a 24-hour period, you would probably not see many marketers changing their listings' positions significantly over the course of the day to reflect a difference in conversion behavior. Perhaps the high bids

163

and positions you see the advertisers using conform with their CPO targets for the full 24-hour period, but I doubt it.

For Yuppiemart, the average conversion rate over the full 24-hour period is 2.875%. That would mean for its most important term, "izod shirt," the company can only afford $1 per click. Thus, Yuppiemart may be stuck in position four. This scenario results in two campaign inefficiencies, as follows:

1. During the peak in traffic, and when the quality of the searcher is greatest, Yuppiemart loses a huge opportunity. If a competitor has search position number two, the searcher may find an appropriate product at that company's website. The tragic part is for that six-hour lunchtime span, Yuppiemart could make money paying for position number two for "izod shirt."

2. Before and after lunch, Yuppiemart might make money in position five, given the 2.5% conversion rate. Then overnight, the only way that Yuppiemart can stay on target with its CPO is in position six, where the CPC is $0.70.

Another alternative would be to simply focus on the lunchtime period exclusively, but then order opportunities during other times of the day might be missed. In addition to implementing day-part campaign optimization, Yuppiemart might find that analyzing the days of the week also uncovers patterns of conversion that can be used to optimize.

Many SEM tools have the capability to assist you in managing by day-part or day of the week. If you have an agency manage your paid SEM campaigns, ask your contacts if day-part optimization is available. Is this kind of analysis easy? No. You need the right tools and right strategic mindset. Is it worth it? Can you afford not to find out?

TRUTH

42

Power segments deliver powerful results

The shopping and buying habits of highly profitable, high-revenue customers are different. So is the mix of products they purchase. Analyses of customer behavior and attitudes indicates that buyer segments have unique needs and preferences. Once segments are identified, common attributes (psychographic and demographic) help marketers name them. They then target profitable customers at as many touch points as possible, including the media they buy.

Psychographics and demographics are great in traditional marketing. TV, radio, print, and even outdoor are all sold based on demographic data supplemented with psychographics. In online media buying, some larger media properties also have user demographic data. This makes it easier for media buyers to decide which media are likely to perform. But online often neglects psychographics and demographics, relying instead only on observed conversion behavior.

One company that's done a lot of research into its customer segments is retailer Best Buy. For Best Buy, its important customer segments are "Barrys," high-end customers who spend to get the best; "Jills," busy moms who want a kid-friendly store environment and often purchase based on staff recommendations; and "Buzzs," tech-savvy early adopters who enjoy the latest in gadgets, often buying after carefully reviewing specifications. Your highly profitable customer segments or subsegments (usually, the 20% who deliver 80% of revenue) are likely very different from Best Buy's segments.

Online often neglects psychographics and demographics, relying instead only on observed conversion behavior.

How does this apply to SEM? If different highly profitable customer segments use different search phrases or keywords, it makes sense to only message to each one differently.

"Buzz" types in "6 megapixel SLR camera." He might respond best to a keyword text ad that highlights the ability to compare several cameras by features. "Jill" is more likely to type in "canon digital camera" after seeing a friend's model. Jill might respond to an ad with more emotion, a benefit statement such as, "Snap and share pictures instantly and easily with a Canon digital camera."

If profitable customer segments can be mapped to keywords, you can message to each in the most appropriate way. You'll meet both their needs and your own. Examine the keywords they use to search to gain insight into the searcher's state of mind, and the demo- or psychographics. You'll create a better user experience and improve campaign efficiency.

Landing pages are also critical to the user experience, as well as to the conversion rate. If you map keywords to different market segments, you'll have a pretty good idea which landing pages to test on that keyword (instead of testing all possible pages).

Buzz might respond well to a landing page that offers specifications and allows him to sort and compare cameras based on different product details. Jill might want to see the top seller for her search and respond well to a landing page that discusses it.

Without understanding customer segments, you could arrive at the best landing pages through a structured testing protocol. But wouldn't it be nice to get there faster through segmentation? A full analysis to determine the profitable segments might take time. The sales and account teams might already have a good idea of the segments and their definitions. Tap the knowledge and use it to enhance all your marketing, including SEM.

What are your most valuable audience segments?

Beyond keywords, search engines give you a very powerful array of segmentation technologies you can use to segment your audience. Geographic segmentation might be the most powerful method of segmentation you have, and it is available from all three of the big engines. Why run a campaign nationally when you can custom-tailor campaigns for each region you serve?

Day-parting (time of day/day of week) is another important segmentation lever at your disposal. Additionally, your visitors might display profoundly different buying behavior dependant on your network click source. For example, visitors from AOL demonstrate markedly higher conversion rates for certain offers than those arriving from other ISPs. Demographic segmentation is another exciting tool that the search engines are rolling out, both for search (Microsoft) and content networks (Google).

The real power comes when you overlay these segmentation technologies to identify your best prospects. For example, a certain demographic segment, arriving from a known geographical region at a specific time of day, might have a superb conversion ratio, and by focusing on reaching this segment, you can achieve both higher ROI and afford to bid higher to attract more volume. For example, if the conversion of nonsegmented (mixed traffic) averages 1.5% and the conversion rate from the Chicago DMA is 2.1%, you can afford to bid more than 25% higher. In Microsoft, you could further segment, for example, men aged 26–35 if they index high.

Customer segments are searching. They want your attention. They want to spend, if you speak their language. Know who they are, provide the right products and services, recognize and meet their needs in a way that makes sense to them, and you will succeed.

TRUTH

43

Better account structures deliver better results

Your PPC account with the major engines consists of a few different levels. It's important to keep these levels in mind because different functions are managed at different places.

In Google, you manage your contact and billing information at the account level. Each account can contain up to 25 different campaigns. At the campaign level, advertisers set geographic targets, language preferences, network distribution preferences, and daily budget. Each campaign contains up to 100 different AdGroups. An AdGroup is a group of keywords for which the same ad copy appears. Advertisers can assign maximum CPCs at the AdGroup level or keyword level. (Landing pages are assigned to individual keywords.)

Structurally, there are two key differences between Yahoo! and Google. The first is that, in Yahoo!, daily budgets are managed at the account level, not the campaign level. The other big difference with Yahoo! is the Campaign Optimization feature, which allows for automated bid price optimization by Yahoo!, with the advertiser setting a maximum CPC at the AdGroup or campaign level and giving Yahoo! leeway to raise bid prices by a certain percentage based on performance. Google does not have this feature. Advertisers who opt out of Campaign Optimization can manage their maximum CPCs at the keyword level.

There are also two key differences between Google and Microsoft. Microsoft allows advertisers to boost their bidding for certain targeting parameters, including the time of day and day of week, geographic location of the searcher, and demographic information such as age or gender. These bid-boosting tactics enable advertisers to appear in a high position for their best audience, and in a low position for less-likely prospects. This bid-boost feature is most important for larger advertisers who have a strong preference for a specific target demographic.

Search ad distribution

The top-tier PPC engines—Google, Yahoo!, and Windows Live Search (formerly MSN)—have three categories of distribution outlets. First is "pure" search distribution, in which the marketers' ads appear only on the primary search engine's results pages—google.com, yahoo. com, live.com, and so on.

Second is search syndication partner distribution. Many of the search engines syndicate their results across the Web. Google, for instance, provides the search results for AOL, and Yahoo! powers the search results for CNN.com.

Third is contextual distribution, in which marketers' ads appear on a network of publisher sites. Your ads appear on pages within that network that feature your ad's keywords, which create a logical context for your ad. Google's contextual distribution program is called AdSense, and Yahoo!'s is called Content Match.

Is syndication beneficial to your campaign? There are pros and cons. On the "pro" side, advertising on syndication sites broadens your reach significantly—you've achieved a full-scale engine expansion, at the click of a button. In the case of engine syndication, that also means having the opportunity to get your ad in front of populations that might be uniquely valuable, in ways that set them apart from the population that's looking at the larger engines. For example, Google syndicates its advertising to AOL, and the baby boomer-heavy AOL offers very different opportunities from the more generic Google.

> ...advertising on syndication sites broadens your reach significantly— you've achieved a full-scale engine expansion, at the click of a button.

For the contextual advertising on publisher sites, this also means capturing searchers at a different phase in the buy-cycle. Search advertisers are ready to make a purchase, meaning they're a great customer to advertise to if you want to bring in a sale, but aren't the best customers to look to for creating early buy-cycle excitement. Contextual advertising can fill in that gap in your media mix by reaching out to customers who haven't searched yet, while using keywords to provide the relevance usually associated with search.

But although there are benefits, you need to be careful of your search syndication campaign. For starters, you can't assume that because your ad worked well in Google, it will also work well in AOL. Every engine is different and might need to be treated differently. And unfortunately, you can't specify which engines you'd like to syndicate to and which you wouldn't. For example, if you find that your ads are performing well on AOL and Ask.com, but poorly on Google, you currently cannot boost your bids only on the syndication partners. Similarly, the inability to opt out means that if you're getting a poor ROI on Google but a great ROI on its syndication partners, your overall AdWords campaign will probably have a poorer ROI than you would prefer. Worse still, there's very little you can do about it. You are buying a package of traffic.

And when you consider contextual advertising on publisher sites, the differences between the engines and the syndicated partners becomes even more pronounced. That's because, again, publisher sites attract searchers at the beginning of the buy-cycle, as opposed to the engines, which attract searchers who are already in "hunt mode." Although your contextual search advertising might benefit your branding campaign, it's harder to get measurable ROI from a contextual campaign at the level that you'll get from a pure search campaign. As a branding channel, you need to weigh the value of your contextual search campaign not against the rest of your search efforts, but against your branding efforts.

TRUTH

44

Creating new PPC search landing pages

Are you trying to sell to your customers from your headquarters? If so, you're shortchanging your customers—and yourself. Imagine that you—a potential consumer of products or services from the Gap, GE, Citigroup, and Verizon—have walked into the headquarters of each firm. Your experience would be vastly different from that provided by a selling environment painstakingly designed to cater to your needs while moving you toward eventual purchase. If such environments are well-designed, they'll offer just the right amount of information in both retail and B2B touch points.

Yet many SEMs use their existing sites to sell to searchers along with everyone else. Each searcher has a unique set of needs, but receives an identical user experience. This approach might not seem bad for Gap.com, which is first and foremost an online store. But if your site has evolved from static brochureware, it's difficult to shake off the trappings of those original sites, particularly when a web presence has to serve multiple constituents.

Your site might have been originally designed (and perhaps redesigned several times) to address the information needs of prospects, returning customers, the press, analysts (investment or industry), your reseller, the distributor channel, your in-house staff (as a resource), investors (if public), and perhaps influencers (who don't purchase, but can influence the sale).

Search is critically important for most businesses, because people are increasingly using search engines at every stage of the buying cycle. If search is important for your business, you should probably stop selling to your search visitors from your headquarters. Start thinking like your search visitors, and design a user experience that balances your need to sell against their desires to select the best solution for their needs.

...design a user experience that balances your need to sell against their desires to select the best solution for their needs.

Although nearly every marketer understands the strength of my argument, internal obstacles often conspire to prevent them from taking appropriate action. Many protest that their IT departments and tech teams are resource-constrained and that it might take years to add additional pages to their sites. Fortunately, micro-sites enable you to provide a more personalized user experience without imposing any real burden on your internal operations.

The micro-site solution

A micro-site is a search-specific web presence that includes features and functionality appropriate for targeting searchers. It's highly likely that you've seen some micro-sites, particularly if you've searched within education, credit card, mortgage, cable/satellite, or cell phone markets. B2B and general lead-generation markets are also chock-full of highly focused micro-sites, providing minimal distractions and just enough information to get visitors excited.

Micro-sites need not involve your IT department at all (assuming you have the latitude to test marketing campaigns without their blessing). Most search marketing agencies have departments, technology, and expertise specifically designed to help marketers develop such micro-sites. Even if your IT team is fully behind your micro-site project, it might still make sense to use the tools and technologies developed by your search agency instead of pulling together what you need from different technology vendors and having your IT team integrate it all for the first time.

Search marketing agencies aren't the only players offering expertise in deploying micro-sites. Performance-based and lead-generation firms have made great strides in developing them, too. Many affiliate marketers have also become quite accomplished at developing and deploying micro-sites.

Leveraging search-specific selling

Micro-sites eliminate unnecessary navigation, particularly the kind that threatens transforming your selling/prospect marketing site into your headquarters. You can likely dispense with such content sections as "Press," "About Us," "Employment/Jobs," and other superfluous links and navigation, which your prospects will have little interest in.

You might wonder what makes a search-focused micro-site different from a traditional media-focused micro-site. After all, the same rationale that's generally important for a micro-site is equally valid for any sales and marketing-focused site. Some factors that are often unique to a search-specific micro-site are the following:

- **Ability to leverage search scent**—Searchers are looking for something very specific. A micro-site can effectively use customization technology to serve up a landing page that meets the searcher's specific needs.
- **Engine-specific or geo-specific offers**—Knowing the originating engine or geographical location lets you provide an optimized marketing message.
- **Buy-funnel messaging**—Searchers in the early, middle, or late stages of the buying funnel use different keywords. Your micro-site should be programmed to automatically serve up customized messages to effectively move them through this funnel.

Right now, with the economic climate increasingly uncertain, you can use all the conversion leverage and sales volume you can get. But you might need to invest a bit of time and money to create a PPC search user experience that embraces the searcher's intent, instead of ignoring it. There's no better time to marshal your resources (internally and externally) and use a micro-site to pump up your conversion rates.

TRUTH

45

How to make landing pages better

In ads, keywords combined with powerful, compelling copy are a killer combination. However, if the landing page doesn't follow through on the key points made in the ad, chances rise that visitors will hit the dreaded Back button. You'll pay for a click but get very little, if any, value. If the ad promotes low pricing or free shipping, meet that expectation on the landing page. You might need to shift around copy or layout on the landing page to improve the stickiness of that page for the searcher.

The first thing the searcher sees after clicking on your paid or unpaid search engine link is your landing page. How that landing page performs is one of the keys to a positive ROI from search marketing. High ROI on an SEM campaign hinges on achieving the right mix of pre-click variables and post-click conversion behavior. Pre-click variables such as search venue, position, and offer/creative have an impact on post-click behavior. But even with those variables optimized, there is huge room for campaign ROI improvement.

High ROI on an SEM campaign hinges on achieving the right mix of pre-click variables and post-click conversion behavior.

The next place to look for ROI improvement is the landing page and the site. For example, if your existing conversion to sale ratio is 3% and your allowable CPO (what you are willing to allocate in marketing spending to get a sale) is $30, you can afford to pay only $0.90 CPC in the venue that provides that conversion rate. (Conversion rates on the same keyword change by venue.) The $0.90 maximum bid might not give you the volume you want, leaving you in a low average position. Now imagine that a change to your landing page, site structure, or shopping cart process changes conversion positively. At a 4% conversion rate, your campaign can now be adjusted to pay as much as $1.20 CPC and still be at your target CPO. At 5%, you can afford up to a $1.50 CPC.

Imagine all the campaign flexibility an increased conversion rate delivers. How can this landing page magic be accomplished? What variables on a landing page and site influence your particular type of visitor? Places to start include copy, product images, merchandising, color, visual use of brands, site navigation, shopping cart ease of use, pricing, alternative conversion paths (for example, collecting a name in case the buyer is not ready to buy, or leading the buyer through testimonials or continued selling/education), and a host of other things.

Copy is critical both for the search engine listings and the landing pages and can drive that free organic traffic that is oh-so-wonderful. A good strategy to write copy for landing pages, both for spiders and humans, is to use the inverted pyramid style. This is borrowed from journalist writing, in which one starts with the conclusion, and then follows with the strongest statements supporting that conclusion. If an editor must cut, she can cut from the bottom without losing much impact. Similarly, a reader can come away with a solid idea of the story thesis from the first paragraph.

Sometimes conversions for the exact same keyword can vary dramatically depending on whether the landing page is a category landing page or product landing page. For example, for the keyword phrase "cat toy," I can think of many types of landing pages that would all be acceptable to the engines—some with a single product, some with multiple products, and others listing cat toys by category. What's the perfect landing page for your traffic? Only testing will yield the answer.

Perhaps your site is simply ugly and turns off visitors visually. When considering a redesign that includes a publishing or e-commerce platform, consider one where changes to product templates, category templates, and navigation are fairly easy to make. That way, if you find an improved landing page, you can roll it out globally or in appropriate sections.

Marketing always has room for improvement, and as long as the cost of the improvement justifies the investment, that improvement should be made. Make sure you have an internal or external data collection infrastructure that enables you to measure appropriate data, including pathing, exit pages, and conversion. Finally, put that data to work. Use your improved landing pages to maximize sales while maintaining ROI.

TRUTH

46

Best practices for landing page excellence

You have only a few moments to convince people who've clicked on your ad that your company can meet their needs. Here are some tips for making sure your landing page actually converts the folks you've paid the search engine to deliver.

Messaging—How much copy is on your landing pages? How much is right? Some products or services lend themselves to longer copy, and others work better with short. Copy style is also critical—remember to define a tone, voice, message, structure, and personality appropriate to the product and brand essence.

Merchandising—What images accompany the product or service offering? With apparel, for example, images of the product might include a model who's wearing your apparel; others might be shot against a solid background. Test different images that showcase the product. Try different image sizes. Image quality also has real impact—if images look inferior, a visitor might assume the product is inferior as well.

Also consider the different systems, both visually and technologically speaking, that you use to display products. If a product is available in many colors, swatches or color blocks under the image might improve conversion; you should also consider a more sophisticated color selector that showcases the product in each available color. Meanwhile, some companies are experimenting with advanced image solutions, such as 3-D rotation. Others add a pop-up, enabling shoppers to view a larger version of the same image without leaving the page.

At the same time, keep in mind that prettier isn't always better. There are many cases in which marketers revamp their entire web sites to produce a new, sleek look only to learn through testing that the "ugly" site converted better than the new one had. There are a million reasons why that might be the case; one is simply that a less attractive layout might be more usable for a rushed shopper; another might be that there are still more dial-up users than you think, and their slower download speeds make pretty pages less functional for them.

Price display—Consider testing how pricing is displayed. Do customers respond better to a list price crossed out with a discount price next to it, or simply the discount price alone? How large is the price on the page? If your organization is known for aggressive pricing, these changes could result in significant lift. An important point to keep in mind if an offer is used in search ad creative: Make sure this offer is highly visible on the landing page. Most of the search engines demand this anyway. Nonetheless, you can imagine the annoyance of a searcher who gets excited about an offer and then doesn't see the capability to follow through on it.

Navigation—Do your landing pages display full site navigation, or just the bare bones? Which navigation options are best for search visitors? Sometimes, too many options can derail a sale. Not enough choices might not be adequate for a searcher who wants to do some research before making a purchase.

Abandonment—Any time a visiting shopper abandons the shopping experience, the sale is likely lost forever. There are professionals who specialize in isolating and improving the sales checkout process, along with tools that can make the job easier. Conversion marketing specialist Allison Tucker, of Customer Finders, says, "It's essential to use some website analytics solution to monitor, test, and optimize the users' shopping navigation path to reduce the cart abandonment rate." Which tool you use depends on the other features you require of a web analytics tool. But whatever you use to track your shopping cart success, realize that shopping cart improvement is pure revenue.

> Any time a visiting shopper abandons the shopping experience, the sale is likely lost forever.

Cross- and Up-Sell—Are you cross selling to other products? Do you up-sell accessories? Any marginal revenue or profit derived through cross- or up-selling falls straight to the bottom line. Retail salespeople understand that better than anyone. So should your site designer.

Product reviews—Many retailers find that customers get a big help from customer- or third-party product reviews. Are these features your site should consider? Would they provide a boost if they appeared somewhere on the landing page for, say, a search for a very specific product?

Leave 'em wanting more—One often-overlooked element of your landing page is the value it can offer to people who don't stay on your site to convert. Bryan and Jeffrey Eisenberg advise that you put easily recognizable branding everywhere on your site. That way, someone who lands on your site and exits quickly will still have a brief brand interaction. That might lead to a conversion down the road.

The white-paper effect—Even I was unprepared for the difference in conversion on my company's site after we offered a white paper download. We'd offered a newsletter subscription, but after adding the white paper, conversion went up seven-fold. Better, 65% of people requesting the white paper also subscribed to the newsletter, a win-win situation!

The audio effect—This was almost as dramatic as the white paper. A client added a nice voiceover to his site. It auto-launches as an audio-enabled Flash animation. Conversions went up 15%. Because he sells licensed software at no marginal cost, bottom-line numbers also rose 15%.

Have a chat—Can online chat, integrated with search engine marketing (SEM), improve conversions, increase order size, or make orders more profitable? Very possibly. If your conversion rate is normally 3% and live chat adds 2%, what's the bottom-line impact? That depends on your business.

Look at the cost of the chat solution and, more important, the labor cost of managing chat sessions. These vary. Some companies employ offshore chatters; others use local trained staff. Then, take the profit on chat's conversion rate (long-term or immediate profit, depending on your preference), and calculate net profit. The lift in net profit can enhance the bottom line in two ways, depending on whether you're a pure-play direct marketer or a fixed-budget marketer.

TRUTH

Beyond search: Keyword-targeted media taps the power of Google's AdSense

If you're like many marketers, you've had limited success with the Google content network. Given the improvements Google has made over the last year, you might want to give the content network another look, particularly if you've been running Google content campaigns using the same campaign structure used in your search campaign. Using the same campaign structure for both might not represent the right strategy and implementation to capture the interest of a content user.

Although Google does provide for the delivery of graphical display advertising through its content network, most of you don't have graphical media (ad creative) handy, nor do you have the resources or the inclination to produce the banners needed to run display media in Google's or another's network. If you want to leverage high levels of incremental visibility, clicks, and content, your primary option is good old text links, served contextually. If you're lucky, you can even justify your increased keyword-targeted spending by managing your campaign to the same ROI metrics used for your search campaign.

Google's AdSense provides huge additional reach, but the conversion rate on contextual traffic is often dramatically lower on the content networks than from pure search. Even with separate campaigns and Google's smart-pricing algorithms supposedly bringing things into line, taking effective advantage of the content network is often challenging. Growing a campaign and extracting additional profitable clicks from the keyword-targeted media ecosystem are never easy. However, after your pure search campaign has gone through several iterations of expansion and tuning, the only way (other than fighting a bidding war and raising bids while ROI drops) is to expand the campaign by trying (or retrying) content targeting.

Content is not search. So, if you've tested and continue to use the same campaign structure for content that works well in search,

...if you've tested and continue to use the same campaign structure for content that works well in search, you might be missing huge opportunities.

you might be missing huge opportunities. To maximize reach and opportunity, you need to treat content differently because

- Consumers who are surfing aren't searching. Ads are incidental to the content being consumed. Thus, there's no search scent to craft ads around. The surfers aren't looking for a keyword and scanning the page the way they do in a search engine results page (SERP). Consumers aren't as likely to be in the final stages of the buying cycle, so the ad copy that works in search might not be the optimal ad copy for content-driven advertising. Try different ads in a contextual environment to retune your campaign.

- Contextual advertising is targeted at the AdGroup level, not the keyword level. This means your account structure might not be optimal. Certain combinations of keywords within AdGroups might work particularly well or appeal to the Google targeting engine.

- Google gives content ads a different Quality Score. So any changes you make to improve perceived relevance of the ads in a contextual environment helps lower costs and increase click volume simultaneously.

- You can create different mixes of AdGroups with similar keyword and creative to capture a greater number of impressions due to the AdGroup-targeting feature in Google. For example, you can add keywords, combine them, add synonyms, create phrases, and change match types (although Broad Match may deliver the greatest impression volume). There's actually a firm, AdMetrica, which specializes in creating lots of iterations of a Google content campaign to garner additional volume. You can do initial testing of this concept yourself.

- Your landing page, which was tested and tuned for the search visitor, might not have the optimal mix of information for a visitor from a contextual ad. Consider what a browser might want to learn compared to a shopper closer to making a decision.

- You can apply segmentation modeling to the new contextual tests just as you would with search. For example, perhaps one way to get your metrics into compliance with your targets (cost per lead, cost per order, return on advertising spending, ROI, or other success metric) is to do a day-parting analysis in conjunction with a geo-segmentation analysis. Nearly all the same segmentation tools used in search exist for content ads.

- You can consider site targeting along with all the preceding methods. Some of the sites in Google's network have high volumes and, in conjunction with these methods, you might be able to tune your campaigns to generate the visibility, traffic, and profit you need.

Search inventory is so precious and scarce that we all get a little myopic, focusing our marketing and optimization efforts exclusively on the SERP. However, growing one's business exclusively on search is a game of diminishing marginal returns after a few years. To stimulate your customer's demand instead of simply harvesting it, consider the content network. It's changed a lot recently, and every indication is that it will continue to change. Content is keyword-targeted, which is something we're all used to. We just need to work at getting contextual advertising to work harder for us.

TRUTH

48

Quasi-search: Contextual and behavioral marketing

Advertisers sometimes have difficulty extracting more volume from search. If the problem is due to a lack of inventory, or CPC prices that are hard to justify, consider looking closer at quasi-search media, such as contextual or behavioral. Quasi-search media might help deliver on campaign objectives, whether branding, direct response, or a hybrid of the two.

Over the last several years, lines between search and other targeting methods have blurred. Yet even if PPC search definitions are muddy, particularly among less-sophisticated marketers, search marketing professionals must understand the differences between pure search and other targeting methods. Overall campaign efficiency might depend on understanding the types of quasi-search and how they fit into an integrated campaign that could include other on- and offline media.

Some marketers still view any keyword-targeted media as search, but drawing the line is no longer so easy.

When I ask marketers if they consider keyword-targeted, text-based contextual advertising part of their search budget, they almost always say "yes." The same holds true for behavioral search retargeting when done with text links. When I ask about display advertising that's contextually or behaviorally targeted, answers become more mixed. Some marketers still view any keyword-targeted media as search, but drawing the line is no longer so easy.

Many behavioral targeting systems, which use search as a trigger, group all searchers within a single category to make it easier to buy that traffic in bulk. Removing targeting precision in exchange for volume primarily appeases media buyers willing to trade precision for scale. Sophisticated search buyers must continue to preach the benefits of increasing relevance and control. It's also important to continue to request that engines and media providers give us access to tools that control the level of targeting, so we can make intelligent decisions about how to spend budgets that might be thought of as search but are, in fact, becoming more of an integrated media purchase.

SEM and interactive agencies with strong search skill sets (or even in-house teams that are extremely search savvy) are uniquely positioned to tap the incremental media opportunities that are targeted based on keywords, regardless of whether the targeting methods are contextual or behavioral. Start exploring the behavioral and contextual media opportunities when one or more of the following are true:

- You find it difficult to extract more value from pure search and have gone through several performance-enhancing iterations of expansion and segmentation.
- You're in a highly competitive category.
- Although the primary focus is on direct response, you also build awareness and want to influence consumers toward your brand.
- You have high levels of combined organic and paid search traffic (which can be utilized for retargeting the site's existing search traffic).
- You have an agency or technology that can monitor the interaction effects between pure search and the quasi-search media of behavioral and contextual.
- Your agency or technology can optimize the contextual or behavioral buys in conjunction with the search buy to assure the interaction effects are properly accounted for.

At a recent Search Engines Strategies conference, I had the privilege of sitting with several speakers on a panel dedicated to exploring opportunities within behavioral search retargeting. We discussed optimism in respect to the size of the behavioral search retargeting market and showed how improved targeting based on behavioral search can result in improved relevance for the consumer over broader contextual or channel-based targeting methods while delivering targeting benefits to the advertiser.

As search engines, publishers, and third-party networks roll out more sophisticated contextual and behavioral media options that are keyword-driven, budgets flow into anything marketers consider search. Most marketers consider both contextual and behavioral retargeting of search to be within the search budget. SEM agencies and the skill sets they provide will be increasingly necessary as part of overall online media plans. Evidence of this fact is the continuing acquisitions of SEM firms by general interactive advertising agencies and ad-holding companies.

Regardless of where the line is eventually drawn between search and other media targeted based on keywords, concepts, or behavior, the skills, strategies, and best practices we learn in PPC search campaign management will be highly valuable over the next several years. Even in the midst of economic turmoil, the future looks bright.

TRUTH

49

Behavioral marketing: Behaviorally retargeting searchers

If you were to ask most Internet marketers where their highest-quality clicks originate, many of them would say SEM—and with good reason. The searcher has asked the search engine for specific information and is in a hunt mode for that information. Bid prices are nice and high for Google and Yahoo! because search visibility and those search clicks are increasingly recognized as valuable.

Wouldn't it be great if you could double, triple, or quadruple the clicks you got from your best performing keywords? Well, perhaps you can through the latest spin on PPC search: behaviorally retargeting searchers across the Net. Before we delve into this newer form of ad targeting, I'll review some of the driving forces that make this a potential killer app.

Behaviorally retargeting searchers allows marketers to follow a searcher around the Web.

Where we've been

The problem for search marketers and search publishers is searchers don't spend much time searching (and clicking) as on their other online activities. Most or all of their time is spent reading and absorbing other content, including email, blogs, magazines, and news. On branded properties, publishers judge much of the textual and graphical content Web surfers consume as premium site content. This inventory is sold directly by a sales force on the assumption that everyone can agree the site's premium content attracts a specific type of audience. On these recognizable sites, the ad units (particularly premium placement) are often sold based on demographic, psychographic, or general macro-level profile data of site users (for example, third-party data sources). But the rest of the inventory is sold differently.

That's where search and context come in.

Recently, an increasing percentage of nonpremium inventory has been sold through networks based on contextual targeting, particularly Google's AdSense and the Yahoo! Publisher Network (YPN). Of course, before there was contextual targeting, there were site categorizations or "channels" that could be used to buy and sell media opportunities in a network environment.

Text-advertising opportunities based on channel or subject matter designations have expanded dramatically as well. Kanoodle, which had a channel-based targeting strategy for text links, has been joined by Blogads, AdBrite, Federated Media, and others. Each has its own spin on categorizations, context, and channels.

Much of the ad inventory you see won't generate the publisher much money based on channel or contextual targeting. This caused the rise of behavioral targeting (targeting ads based on prior behavior, such as a past visit to a particular site). Most behavioral ad targeting thus far has been graphical advertising driven through the ad networks and the portals.

Where we're going

The behavior we search marketers care about most is search behavior. Now we have a new big idea: behaviorally targeting ads based on prior search behavior. Behaviorally retargeting searchers enables marketers to follow a searcher around the Web. When that searcher reaches a page that won't earn the publisher much money based on channel, context, or nonsearch behavior, an ad specifically addressing the prior search behavior is served. Wow!

For most keywords, a marketer would be ecstatic to get a 10% conversion rate, but that means 90% of searchers don't convert within that initial search session. Because search behavior is such a great indicator of what a searcher wants, behaviorally retargeting against search behavior creates a win-win-win scenario. The publisher makes more money on inventory that was difficult to sell at a high rate; the searcher sees a really relevant ad instead of another irrelevant one. Most important, we marketers have an opportunity to retarget a person who is in-market for our product or service.

There are two ways you can tap into the power of behavioral search. The first is through the networks and technology providers that work with the networks. The primary players on the network side are Revenue Science, Tacoda, Advertising.com, and AlmondNet.

With the networks, you can retarget based on searchers who have visited your site already, either through paid search or (if you pixel your site) based on organic search. This kind of retargeting is perfect, because those who see the ads already know who you are. The downside of the network model is you get to talk only to those searchers you already talked to before. And due to third-party cookie deletion, over time you won't be able to reach much of your pre-targeted audience.

If my predictions hold true, the second way you'll be able to take advantage of behavioral search is through the search engines themselves on a CPC basis. Yahoo! has had a CPM retargeting product called Impulse for years, which might interest some marketers now. Google, Yahoo!, and MSN haven't yet announced any CPC-based behavioral search products, but they're in a great position to do so. The best thing about the engines getting into behavioral retargeting is they know every search a searcher engages in and don't have to wait until that searcher visits your site. They can retarget a searcher who might have visited your competition. Also, the cookies search engines use to retarget are far less likely to be deleted, meaning searchers can see relevant ads for a longer period.

I'm excited by the possibilities that behaviorally retargeting searchers will provide for marketers, which is why we've been testing it. This could be the year of behavioral search advertising if all three major search engines roll out products to join the ad networks in providing this option. You might suddenly be able to spend twice as much on search advertising by reaching your searchers after they complete their review of the SERP. Email use alone could be a tremendous location for behavioral search ads. All three search engines have huge email bases (Gmail, Hotmail, and Yahoo! Mail), as well as large content areas that they own or control. That's powerful.

TRUTH

50

Keywords are not enough for B2B marketing

One of the greatest challenges with business-to-business (B2B) search marketing campaigns is that many keywords aren't pure B2B. In fact, the keyword lists used by many B2B marketers are appropriate for attracting both businesses and consumer searchers. And the ambiguous search results resulting from these lists pose challenges for marketers and searchers alike.

These keywords also create problems for search engines, because they're in the business of providing quality search results. If a searcher types "tempered glass" or "switching power supply," the engines can't know if the searcher wants business- or consumer-oriented information. Of course, most B2B marketers don't sell directly to consumers, so this type of situation poses a challenge for all involved.

Chances are that B2B marketers will be receiving at least some consumer traffic on ambiguous search terms.

This truth covers strategies that B2B marketers can implement to build more profitable businesses, despite these built-in ambiguities.

Prequalify searchers

Web portals are places that typically bring together information from a variety of different sources to serve as a primary "start" page for users. Not all portals serve both consumers and businesses. Business.com, the Thomas Register, and other "vortals" (vertical portals) can be used to prequalify searchers as B2B by their nature. B2B marketers should certainly consider steps to gain visibility in any vortal covering their industries.

Business.com is a great choice for almost all industries. In 2004, the Thomas Global Register launched ThomasB2B.com, a directory encompassing some 700,000 manufacturers and distributors. Search listings are auctioned using FindWhat.com's back-end technology. If Thomas Register's audience is right for you, consider one of its full listing plans that includes CD-ROM, print, and Internet distribution.

Three more strategies

Vortals, however, don't get the majority of B2B traffic. Most commercial B2B search queries probably originate through the major portals (Yahoo!, MSN, AOL.com, and so on) by searchers who either prefer that portal or don't know that vortals exist. To capture this kind of qualified traffic, you need to plan, execute, and optimize a campaign in the major portals to complement a vortal strategy.

In Yahoo!, you might try changing copy to make listings less ambiguous. For example, if you sell cleaning supplies only in large quantities to janitorial companies and landlords, your listing title could begin with "Bulk Wholesale Cleaning Supplies." In Google, it's riskier to prequalify B2B clickers with titles or descriptions to clarify offerings as being B2B when a keyword is searched by both consumers and businesses. A low CTR on a Google ad results in a lower position for a given CPC. Having a low CTR may also result in the delivery of ads being slowed or even disabled. Consequently, you may need to find Google creative that's relevant for the majority of the searchers, business or consumer.

Chances are that B2B marketers will be receiving at least some consumer traffic on ambiguous search terms. In this case, the best option is to figure out whether you have an alternate use for the consumer traffic your listings generate. There are several strategies you can implement, depending on the nature of your business. The key to a B2B search strategy is to evaluate your overall sales and marketing plan and determine if the following search strategies make sense:

- Do you plan to support your distribution channel? If you sell hard drive arrays to Value-Added Retailers (VARs), retailers, and mail order firms, why not devote some landing page real estate to links or messaging about consumer purchase options? The click is paid, so you might as well support your channel.
- Send consumer searchers to a dealer locator page.
- Send consumers to partner, retailer, or VAR sites. To quantify this benefit internally and to your channel, have your web team use outbound click-counter redirects to quantify traffic you provide to each entity in your channel. (A *redirect* is an indirect link to another site, not an untrackable direct link.)

- Do you have a division that sells small quantities directly? If you sell direct to consumers as a smaller segment of your business, use some landing page real estate to direct consumers to your retail site.
- If you're interested in establishing a dialogue with end-user consumers, offer a newsletter sign-up or another carrot to encourage them to register on your site. Once a dialogue is established, you might be able to channel eventual demand for your product to the appropriate channel.

B2B marketers with ambiguous keywords in their campaigns can prosper using creative strategies along with site development and landing page optimization that keep consumer and business searcher needs in mind. Take a fresh look at your campaign. Are you sorting ambiguous traffic to get your money's worth?

TRUTH

51

B2B search best practices

Online retailing, financial services, and travel get a lot of attention when it comes to Internet and search marketing. What isn't mentioned as much is another hot area in search marketing: business-to-business (B2B).

B2B marketers know that the value of a new customer is typically very high. Individual transaction sizes are high, and once an affiliation has been forged, the business relationship's lifetime value can be in the hundreds, thousands, or even millions of dollars. That makes search a particularly critical part of many B2B marketing managers' overall marketing plans. Regardless of where prospects are in the buying cycle, chances are search is part of their daily routine. Among other things, prospects may be researching the following:

> **Regardless of where prospects are in the buying cycle, chances are search is part of their daily routine.**

- Capabilities
- Specifications
- Usage practices
- Reliability issues
- Costs (including costs of ownership and maintenance)
- Liability issues
- Substitutability with other products or services
- Manufacturer reputation
- Testimonials or case studies
- Supplier/distributor locations

A well-crafted paid search and organic search marketing plan makes sure the site's content meets the needs of visitors seeking this type of information.

When managing CPC- or CPM-based search marketing campaigns, remember that not every visitor is in the same place in the buying cycle. When measuring, managing, and optimizing a campaign, you might want to set blended objectives that go beyond a simple "contact us" lead form or a phone call.

Those searchers in earlier phases of the buying cycle might download white papers, look up specifications, use product configuration wizards, or take any multitude of actions on your site.

In some user actions, such as registrations, the identity of the visitor is captured. Other actions will be anonymous but still might tell you something about that visitor's value. By assigning each post-click behavior and action a relative value based on your business, your campaign can be optimized to take into account the true value of visitors.

Think about your business, your sales cycle, and the way visitors to your site interact with the content, as well as which calls to action you have built into the site. You might even want to place different calls to action on your site, to appeal to various types of prospects.

> If you're trying to attract searchers in a particular phase of the buying cycle, tune your copy appropriately.

The way you use copy in your B2B listings is also critical. If you're trying to attract searchers in a particular phase of the buying cycle, tune your copy appropriately. Be aware that for your industry, consumer marketers might share some keywords. The keyword "lumber" might be searched by both businesses and consumers, whereas "lumber kiln" or "hardwood lumber molding" are more likely to be business searches.

When a term is ambiguous, your creative strategy must be tuned based on the venue. Because of how it looks at relevance, Google may penalize your ad if your copy prequalifies the searcher, particularly when other ads competing for the traffic are not doing so. Similarly, Yahoo!'s "Click Index" can get an ad removed if the CTR falls too low in comparison to neighboring ads.

As with all online marketing, hone and test landing pages to assure a good fit with the creative and search term, as well as the expected visitors' needs. A landing page that does well for one phrase might not work well for others.

In addition to the expected paid search listings locations, , there are also specific B2B portals (some of which cover specific vertical markets). Most of these vertical portals sell listings on an annual or CPC basis. Those alternate search listings vendors go far beyond what your might expect. They include the following:

- Thomas Register (manufacturers and distributors)
- Bitpipe (white papers for IT)
- Business.com (general vertical business search)
- The Internet Yellow Pages at Yahoo!, Verizon SuperPages.com, and so on
- Respond.com (personal and professional services)
- Lawyers.com (personal and business users)
- Enterprise Software HQ (requests for proposals and quotes)

Many of these alternate sources of search traffic have monthly, annual, or hybrid deals instead of the CPC deals you might be accustomed to getting with the major search portals. In addition, some have prospects fill out lead forms. As a marketer, you have the option of purchasing these leads on a per-name basis. Depending on the vendor, those leads might be exclusive by geography or prequalification, so measure the long-term value of leads, particularly if that is what you are buying from the venue.

As a B2B marketer, your sales cycle may be long. Therefore, I highly recommend you tag your leads with a code that indicates the source by engine/vendor, keyword, and possibly even click or lead price. That way, you can do an analysis as sales close and gain an understanding of where the really valuable traffic is coming from. This lead source conversion information might not change your short-term campaign strategy, where lead generation is the primary goal. But in the long term, it sure helps to know where the sales and revenue originate—just in case the CEO comes in and slashes your marketing budget while raising sales goals.

TRUTH

52

Mobile keyword targeting

Mobile search is gaining momentum. Analysts, gurus, and pundits point to massive device adoption overseas. Google, Yahoo!, and Microsoft continue to invest heavily in mobile technology, including ad serving, testing different monetization schemes, and ad formats. But mobile needs to become material and more of a consumer behavior influencer for more people before marketers claim successes.

Clearly, people use mobile search when they need information on the go. If it's a commerce-related search, there's an opportunity to simultaneously meet the searcher's needs and the marketer's objectives. Local businesses, particularly restaurants, bars, movie theaters, and retailers, can present their location or business information to consumers when they're actively searching and proximal to their location. However, not all searches with regional or geographic intent are suitable for mobile ad platforms.

For example, my wife, a psychologist, would probably prefer *not* to get calls from people who decided they need therapy or want to improve their mental health while walking down a nearby street. The same holds true for my accountant. (Some might argue that mobile could be a great platform for medical malpractice or criminal lawyers.)

...there's an opportunity to simultaneously meet the searcher's needs and the marketer's objectives.

As retail websites' interfaces and content become more mobile-friendly, including product-availability searches at specific store locations, mobile use may increase. Still, significant issues remain that the mobile ad industry must solve, including the following:

- **Ad-format challenges**—What's the right ad format for mobile devices? Banners don't render the same across all devices. This is partially due to different screen aspect ratios, as well as browser compatibility challenges that make Firefox/IE incompatibilities seem quaint.

- **Ad-payment/monetization issues**—User behavior on mobile devices is different. Often users want to engage in a call, so PPC doesn't make sense as an ad vehicle. Pay per call has much of the trackability PPC does, a feature that will appeal to many marketers as well as consumers. Click to call, a close cousin to the pay-per-call platform, requires users to enter their number to have the switch initiate the call. This presents a poor user experience in the current mobile environment. SMS-based calls to action have some significant opportunities, particularly when combined with offer codes and coupons.

- **Mobile coupon incompatibility**—Mobile coupons that can be scanned from the phone display may be a killer app. However, it seems barcode laser scanners don't work reliably on mobile device screens, but the pulsed LED scanners do. If this problem is addressed, coupons could be embedded with media-tracking codes.

- **GPS and location-based service (LBS)**—Based on my research, the location of your LBS-enabled cell phone is currently transmitted only to 911 or within a special network, such as Wherify Wireless. But if the benefits of better targeted advertising become great enough, users might opt to have their phones broadcast their location regardless of the Big-Brother factor.

Clearly, we've reached critical mass among early mobile search adopters. If the price for larger-screen phones falls within consumers' reach in their next phone-upgrade cycle, we might see a dramatic uptick in mobile search. But before pursuing mobile search advertising for your business, think about its value to you and mobile consumers. Are they worth more or less than stationary consumers? Let your answer guide your strategy.

TRUTH

53

Social search

News flash! Humans are taking over the Internet! Their weapons are user-generated content and an overlay of human enhancements on top of existing content. An increasing use of social search, combined with the explosion of user-generated content, is changing the Internet's balance of power yet again.

Search engines have always relied on humans to improve result relevancy. Yahoo! started off as a directory. It still employs people to review PPC ad creative before allowing it to go live. Google continues to rely on the user-generated DMOZ open directory project, even though most of the online advertising and SEM industry feel DMOZ is in a state of disarray and needs an overhaul. More recently, Google has been relying increasingly on Wikipedia, a human-entered and human-edited encyclopedia, and has recently launched what it calls Knol, a service similar to Wikipedia that harnesses the power of "crowd-sourcing" to produce useful knowledge.

The resurgence of humans taking over the Internet, and search along with it, is occurring in several areas, particularly social search, social networking, and blogs. Social search is primarily considered an organic SEO phenomenon. Tagging and recommendations become a big relevance factor. However, two major problems arise. The first is that spamming is possible. The second is the self-fulfilling prophecy wherein top results are voted on and recommended more, thus locking them in. Blogs operate in a similar way, with links and comments combining with track-back functionality that creates a voting system that takes advantage of the search engine's link-centric relevancy algorithms.

> Social search is primarily considered an organic SEO phenomenon.

However, some of the voting and tagging information generated by human-generated content could easily find its way into Google's Quality Score, given Google's focus on relevance. Google knows which paid ad listings cause users to return to the original SERP after sampling sites, which results in a "sticky site" visit (defined as the length of time before either returning to the SERP or engaging in another search activity). I wouldn't be surprised to see this information become one of the many Quality Score components used to judge relevancy.

Social networking, on the other hand, will have a huge impact on PPC advertising, particularly contextual and behavioral inventory (which technically isn't PPC search). Already, social networking sites such as MySpace and Facebook are garnering huge amounts of page views. According to comScore, MySpace racked up 45.6 billion page views in May of 2008, with Facebook edging ahead to some 50.6 billion views. That's a lot of inventory, and the search engines want to serve targeted ads across it, which is why Google and Microsoft inked deals to serve ads across them. Regardless of whose network the ad inventory ends up in, as marketers we need to understand whether this inventory is right for us and if we're getting that inventory in our PPC clickstream.

To tell where a click originates from, web analytics, tracking, or campaign management technologies rely on something called the HTTP referrer. Most clicks still have an HTTP referrer. Missing referrers can be caused by a multitude of factors, including the situation where the visitor navigated directly to a page through a bookmark or by directly typing in a URL. Some firewall software strips out the referrer because sometimes there's a security risk caused by a link from a page that includes personally identifiable information in the URL. This becomes visible to the next site visited. Some spyware and adware have no referrer because the click didn't originate from a web page. But most browsers and computers allow passing of the HTTP referrer. By conducting an analysis of PPC traffic, you'll be able to determine if clicks originating at MySpace and the other social networking site are better or worse than other clicks you buy.

Many in the industry believe that as search engine contextual and behavioral traffic grows as a percentage of overall traffic, the engines will have to provide marketers with better control in regard to ads running across sites and other nonsearch networks. An opt-in system that separates the top 20 sites within a network would provide a high level of control for sites delivering a material level of traffic but add significant complexity to an already-complex marketplace. My suggestion to several of the top search engines is to at least provide an opt-out option for domains you don't want to buy traffic from. That way, at least you could minimize future damage to a campaign from sites that delivered traffic that isn't working well without having to entirely shut down a campaign segment.

Here's an example of how an opt-out system might work. If I sell guitar amps and electric guitars and want to tap Google's contextual networks, there might be a ton of really great sites and blogs suitable for running my ads. But my ads might also show up on MySpace, where there are highly interested readers who actually may want my product, but who are 15 years old, who have no credit card, and whose parents aren't going to drop $500 on a Fender amp. By opting out of MySpace traffic, I'd be left with a smaller Google network, one that performs sufficiently well to complement my search campaign. Similarly, I might decide that LinkedIn traffic works particularly well, so I buy it through the Google site-targeting option, bidding a CPM for impressions.

It's too early to determine exactly how the search engines will address the differing kinds of traffic that originate from sites within their ever-growing contextual networks. It will take more than a smart-pricing approach similar to what Google's using now to discount clicks from certain sources, and a lot more transparency as to which ads ran where and reached whom.

TRUTH

54

Are organic search results an endangered species?

It's long been assumed as true among many web users that the organic results served up by the search engines' algorithms are more relevant to most users' queries than the paid results. This perception has largely been manufactured by the search engines themselves, each of which seeks to endear itself to users as an "honest broker" whose neutral algorithms will unerringly separate the wheat from the chaff. Although the idea that organic results are "pure" is an inherently appealing one; in actuality the situation is much more complicated and, in many instances, paid listings actually provide better, more useful results than organic ones.

The first instance in which paid listings consistently provide more relevant results occurs when a user makes a query with local intent— for example, "plumber" or "office cleaning services." In this case, the search engine's ad server automatically geo-targets paid results that are based upon the user's IP address, which is mapped against a location database. So, a user making such a search from New York will see paid listings for New York-based plumbers and janitors. Some engines are also supplementing the IP address geo-targeting with profile-based targeting by using user-volunteered data.

Organic listings, however, do not reflect the user's location unless the user types in an additional term to indicate one, such as "plumber NYC" or "plumber New York." Of course, that organic results aren't geo-targeted might not always produce less relevancy. (If I'm researching the history of plumbing or whether plumbers in the U.S. belong to a union, I won't care about plumbers in my neighborhood.) But for certain queries that clearly demonstrate a local intent, geo-targeted paid listings may deliver more relevancy than organic ones. Google currently shows only a map result when a geography is specified.

The second instance in which paid listings may provide better relevancy is more subtle, and it is a phenomenon caused by systemic structural biases affecting the way organic and paid listings are served. Organic results are, of course, subject to manipulation by wily SEO practitioners who are paid by their clients to secure the best ranking positions for their clients' sites. No one who practices SEO optimization likes to be labeled as cheaters or manipulators, especially because many of them do provide a useful service to

their clients by guiding them toward improving the search engine friendliness of their sites. But some of them will freely admit that they practice tricks and tactics that go beyond simple optimization into the zone of manipulation. For them, the ends (getting top rankings for their clients) justify whatever means they use to trick the engines into thinking that a given site is more relevant than it actually is.

The engines naturally seek to discourage such behavior, and do impose economic disincentives that constrain the optimizers' activities on an ad-hoc basis. The threat of these penalties does serve as a disincentive against extreme "black hat" optimization tactics, but beyond this, it does nothing to enhance relevancy in the organic results space. As a rule, aggressive SEOs go after high traffic terms, regardless of whatever negative impact on relevance such manipulation may have. And this irresistible economic reality is what drives the optimizer's behavior.

At the same time, a very different battle with its own set of economic rules is being waged among marketers running paid search campaigns. Here, each of these marketers seeks the highest possible SERP listings position at the lowest possible keyword acquisition price. Obviously, only one contestant can win this battle at any point in time, and bid price is only one factor determining the winner. In a nutshell, the engines' auctions provide powerful economic incentives for marketers to produce the most compelling, most likely-to-be-clicked-upon, most relevant results. That this result, which maximizes the engines' revenues, happens to accord with users' desire for relevancy, is one of the happier coincidences in the search-marketing industry.

...marketers seeking to advertise with irrelevant terms or with less-than-relevant creativity are often attracting traffic less likely to convert.

Another factor enforcing relevancy in the paid search marketplace is that marketers are penalized for attracting irrelevant traffic. Ironically, marketers seeking to advertise with irrelevant terms or with less-than-relevant creativity are often attracting traffic less likely to convert. For example, if you work

for a law firm that specializes in civil practice, you would not want people looking for criminal defense attorneys to click on your ad. So, it would be foolhardy to bid highly to gain top rankings for the term "lawyer" because you'd be wasting tens, perhaps hundreds of dollars each day paying the engines for clicks of which a high percentage will never convert.

Consequently, two very different sets of incentives and disincentives operate to determine the production of organic and paid search results. One is biased toward relevancy, and the other forces the search engine to proactively fight to maintain relevancy pitted against an army of webmasters and SEO practitioners, all of whom want that "free" top spot for their favorite keywords. Although it is true that top-ranking organic results are rarely totally irrelevant, SEOs can game the system easily enough to manufacture a sense of relevancy that is in fact a phantom. Because there are no built-in penalties for doing so (except when one "crosses the line" and is caught), this practice is rampant and degrades the relevancy of organic results.

With paid search, we have exactly the opposite situation: Marketers are rewarded for enhancing relevancy—not degrading it—which enhances the relevancy of paid results.

TRUTH

55

Search beyond the browser

Search marketing is fundamentally simple. Marketers need to place messages that most closely relate to a user's query in both relevance and position. What makes the process complex is that SERPs provide for more than one message to be placed, and a real-time auction allocates position based on bid. Additionally, in hybrid auctions (systems that the three major engines are already running), various scoring mechanisms influence the bid price. Although each search engine's organic and ad-serving algorithms differ significantly, they all share remarkably common features, beginning with the SERP. Although the presentation of these "answer" pages differs noticeably, at root they contain the same two main content components: organic and sponsored results.

The SERP paradigm of multiple results, quickly disintegrates as the search bar relocates itself from the browser/searcher/clicker model toward other platforms in which the central query/response mechanism will continue to be central—for example, cell phone browsers, in which the 1024×768 browser window is reduced to a tiny fraction of a monitor's screen size. Text size must be proportionally expanded to be readable on these tiny screens, which reduces the number of results that can be displayed per any given query. The use of cell phone browsers will continue to reinforce the pressure on marketers to achieve top-ranked positions, especially as the cost of "not being #1" is far steeper on a cell phone than on a computer monitor.

Search engines are naturally interested in extending their self-serve ad platforms to the cell phone to extend their reach. In early September of 2006, Google began allowing its AdWords marketers to create mobile ads for cellular carriers in Germany (T-Mobile, Vodafone, E-Plus, and O2), the UK (T-Mobile, Vodafone, O2, and Orange), and the U.S. (Cingular, Sprint, Verizon, T-Mobile, and Nextel). Yahoo! has been providing search services since early 2005 for Nokia, and Microsoft has a clear interest in extending adCenter to non-web search platforms.

What's been missing from the equation is a critical mass of users and marketers capable of creating a marketplace. The number of G3 cell phone users in the U. S. is still comparatively small, and only about 10 million people are capable of being exposed to mobile search marketing messages. But industry analysts have forecast robust growth

for mobile marketing: Mobile industry watcher Informa predicts $1.7 billion in revenues for 2007 and up to $11 billion by 2011.

What remains to be seen is whether the carriers will submit to the search engines' desires to extend their empires beyond the pay-as-you-go, bring-your-own-bandwidth Internet. Cell carriers "own" the frequencies, and they want to maximize their share of ad revenues derived from mobile search. Some carriers have clearly articulated that instead of cutting in Google, Yahoo!, or Microsoft on the ad pie, they intend to manage their own ad networks. As a marketer, you need to be watching the mobile market carefully, and take advantage of it sooner rather than later.

The bad news, of course, is that the addition of mobile search capabilities will further complicate the management of your existing and future paid search campaigns.

That mobile advertising might enable marketers to exploit localization technologies—for example, to notify a given user that the restaurant he's walking by has a special on steak sandwiches—has generated a great deal of discussion. This possibility prompts questions such as: How can such a system be smart enough to suppress such advertising if the cell phone user is a vegetarian? For this kind of intelligence to be innate within any such system, much more has to be known about the user than his simple geographical location. Instead, the ability to link location data to historical search query data, voluntarily submitted self-disclosures, and tap into his digital footprint would be a tool of greater value to marketers.

Whoever connects these elements will be able to exert considerable control over the next evolution of digital advertising as it moves into the mobile arena. It is likely that a partnership between carriers and the search engines, which already possess terabytes of information relating to the individual predilections of their customers, will provide the infrastructure for such next-generation mobile advertising platforms.

I believe that, as most mobile devices dial a number when the browser cursor is positioned over it and clicked, one valid form of paid mobile advertising will be Pay-Per-Call. Given the mobile user's likely objectives when conducting a search, this form of monetization might be a better fit than Pay-Per-Click.

Acknowledgments

I would like to thank the entire Didit team, particularly Steve Baldwin, whose editorial expertise continues to be invaluable to me and who helped make sure this book is clear and understandable. In addition, the entire industry, including my ClickZ.com readership and the changing members of the SEMPO Board of Directors, have continued to inspire me to both learn and teach best practices in search engine marketing.

About the Author

Kevin Lee, Didit Founder, Chairman, and CEO, has been an acknowledged Search Engine Marketing (SEM) expert since 1995. Kevin's years of SEM expertise provide the foundation for Didit's proprietary Maestro search campaign technology. Didit's unparalleled results and client growth have earned Didit recognition not only among marketers, but also as part of the 2007 Inc 500 (#137), as well as a #12 position on Deloitte's Fast 500. Kevin's "Paid Search Strategies" column for ClickZ is read by thousands, and his book, *The Eyes Have It: How to Market in an Age of Divergent Consumers, Media Chaos, and Advertising Anarchy*, has been widely praised. A founding board member of SEMPO and its first elected chairman, Kevin is also active on DMA and IAB committees.

The Wall Street Journal, *Business Week*, *The New York Times*, *Bloomberg*, *CNET*, *USA Today*, *San Jose Mercury News*, and other press quote Kevin regularly. Kevin lectures at leading industry conferences, as well as at NYU, Columbia, Fordham, and Pace Universities. Kevin's expertise is also valued by Wall Street; he has briefed analysts and clients of JP Morgan, RBC, UBS, Piper Jaffray, Goldman Sachs, Citicorp, and others. Kevin earned his MBA from Yale School of Management in 1992 and lives in Manhattan. Kevin was recognized as an Ernst & Young Entrepreneur Of The Year® 2008 Award Finalist in Metro New York Area and received the 2008 Direct Marketing Club of New York, Mal Dunn Leadership Award.

In addition, in 2008, Kevin and partner David Pasternack launched a social entrepreneurship venture, www.We-Care.com, a web technology that generates passive donation revenue for nonprofit causes, including schools, universities, associations, clubs, and houses of worship.